Navigating Conflict:
A Guide Through the Storm

Rodney A. Harrison
Jeffrey A. Klick
Glenn A. Miller

What Others Are Saying

To pastor a church is to, on occasion, know conflict. Even the healthiest of churches find themselves in seasons of disruptions, and even the most well–intentioned pastor will find himself embroiled in such conflict sooner or later. Thankfully, *Navigating Conflict: A Guide through the Storm* is a steady resource for pastors and staff ministers who long for unity in the local church, and in sorting through conflict with minimal collateral damage. I am thankful these authors have shared their wisdom and keen insight in this book. I know countless ministries will be blessed.

Dr. Jason Allen
President, Midwestern Baptist Theological Seminary

Thirty-nine years of ministry as a pastor, ecclesial overseer, and educator have given me ample opportunity not only to recognize the conflict examples that these experienced authors share, but also to resonate with the sound advices and strategies contained in this helpful book. Harrison, Klick and Miller are giving us practical and effective strategies for reframing conflict from "occasion for panic" to "opportunity for growth." Prayerfully applied, this book can indeed become "a guide through the storm.

Dr. Jeren Rowell,
President, Nazarene Theological Seminary

Even within Christian circles conflict is inevitable. How we deal with conflict determines the success of our relationships, ministries, and ultimately our testimony. *Navigating Conflict: A Guide Through the Storm,* is a biblical, practical, insightful resource that is an indispensable resource for anyone who is engaged in Christian service. The authors draw from a wealth of experience that brilliantly illustrates the pitfalls, pain, and the promise of successfully dealing with conflict.

Dr. Anthony Allen,
President, Hannibal LaGrange University

Conflict comes to every church at one time or another. *Navigating Conflict: A Guide Through the Storm* is a timely work for any pastor which is in the middle of the battle of raging conflict. Do not miss the third section of this book which speaks of the spiritual side of managing conflict. This is perhaps the greatest contribution of this work. All of us have had to or are about to deal with the Pretenders, Dividers, and Obnoxious People that seek to hurt the Lord's Church. The eighteen red flags of a church antagonist are something every pastor ought to laminate and put in the top drawer of his office desk.

Harrison, Klick, and Miller have been a group of authors I read regularly. They know how to help local churches in the hard stuff of ministry and evangelism. Read this book and put it where you can reach it when the storm of conflict comes. You will never regret it!

Tom Cheyney, Founder, Directional Leader
The Renovate Group
Renovate National Church Revitalization Conferences
Author, Life After Death: A Strategy to Bring New Life to a
Dead Church!

The writers of the New Testament foresaw trouble for believers of the faith, and especially for leaders. If you are taking your Christianity seriously, conflict comes with it. The authors of *Navigating Conflict* know this, and have decided to help the rest of us through the morass of ministry with their years of experience and wise counsel. Those having and inducing conflict have styles, and so do those of us helping them, and to see these patterns come together for Kingdom good is a study worth having. Harrison, Klick and Miller know a few things because they have experienced a few things. Those who take seriously these lessons will be blessed.

Dr. Matt Friedeman
John M. Case Professor of Evangelical Studies
Wesley Biblical Seminary

Disagreements and disputes so often lead to raging storms that cut a swath of relational destruction. *Navigating Conflict* is a must read for anyone who desires to learn and understand how to successfully traverse through the turbulence of conflict. The collective wisdom of the authors will help you confidently pursue a scriptural and practical path toward reconciliation that honors Christ.

Dr. Gary Mathes, Director of Missions,
Clay-Platte Baptist Association

In a day when so much of what we read on the subject seems idealistic or superficial or disconnected from reality, *Navigating Conflict* is full of experiential wisdom, pastoral application, and solid biblical guidance. This book will help the ministry leader step on fewer land mines in his church.

Jared C. Wilson, Assistant Professor of Pastoral Ministry at
Spurgeon College and author of The Gospel-Driven Church

Navigating Conflict is not just another textbook guide to conflict resolution although it is gifted with abundant models, means, and methods for restorative intervention and stewardship. This work dives into the reality that conflict is always "educational", revealing much about ourselves and our organizations. This knowledge helps us steward conflict as an essential component of innovation and growth. If God has placed you where two or more are gathered, read and apply!"

George Townsend, Executive Vice President
Central Seminary

Navigating Conflict is a great tool for helping leaders everywhere work through the inevitable conflict that arises wherever there are people. This is a very practical book and easy to read, with a helpful table of contents to take you right to the chapter you need at the moment!

J. Mark Fox, Instructor, School of Communications,
Elon University, Pastor, Antioch Community Church

In my two decades of pastoral ministry and experience leading teams in Christian higher education, one thing I have learned is that conflict resolution remains one of the most needed, yet underdeveloped, skills. *Navigating Conflict* is a welcome book that defines the problem well. Harrison, Klick, and Miller share their wisdom in a conversational style that makes their practical advice easy to understand and apply. To everyone who has experienced the stabbing pain of betrayal or the aching loss of friendship, *Navigating Conflict* will help mitigate future heartache and find encouragement in the love of Christ.

J.R. Miller, Professor of Applied Theology Leadership at
Southern California Seminary and Author of Elders Lead a
Healthy Family

What an excellent book! *Navigating Conflict* is much more than a book – it is a handbook – a ready and versatile resource for offering a loving approach to most every kind of conflict. What I like most about *Navigating Conflict* is that the authors continually point us to Christ. This book is not about how a leader can manipulate his way to success. No, *Negotiating Conflict* is about learning to exalt Christ in the midst of genuine, even heart-breaking conflict. Continually pointing us to Christian virtues, the authors show us how we can glorify God by humbly leveraging conflict for the glory of God. Thanks to the authors! They have laced their experiences together to fashion an enduring and dynamic ministry tool.

Eric Burd
President Household of Faith Fellowship of Churches

Dedications

For my fellow under-shepherds plugging away day after day serving their King greatly loved by Him. Jeff

To my MM staff who serve diligently and faithfully, and who challenge me weekly and keep me humble every day! Bless you all! Glenn

To the churches, small and large, who keep making disciples and evangelizing the lost. Rodney

Special Thanks

We would like to pass on a very special thanks to our wives and family, for your unwavering support and love. We would also like to thank Chris Miller for the cover design, Bobbie Crane for editing, C.J. Moore, Doctoral Fellow for his assistance in research. and to our Lord Jesus for loving and redeeming us from the curse of sin.

Contents

Foreword

God designed and wired us for community and connection. Humans are overwhelming their happiest and at their best when they are connected to each other in safe high-trust relationships.

Conflict undermines our ability to connect. Brothers and sisters in Christ connecting at a meaningful level is the lifeblood of a church, or at least it should be!

Often unmanageable conflict keeps us as individuals and the church as whole from reaching our God given redemptive potential. If you have at least two people in your church, conflict is unavoidable.

Modern neuroscience has opened a whole new world of understanding about how the brain works and responds to threats both real and imagined. In short, we have full access to our prefrontal cortex, the seat of reason and sound judgement, when we do not feel threatened. Faced with threats like conflict, sudden change, or big decisions, the amygdala cuts off the blood flow to the prefrontal cortex and redirects it to the primitive brain or reptile brain. This area of the brain triggers the flight or fight response. This can often be witnessed at the church business meeting.

At a deep level, often undetected by the person being affected by it, the phenomenon is not only triggered by physical threats but anything that threatens our self-worth, status, creates uncertainty, undermines our autonomy or seems unfair.

The truth is almost anything can set us off flooding our bodies with heavy doses of cortisol - the chemical that makes us fight. Once our reptile brain takes over, we often act and behave in ways that simply don't serve ourselves or others well.

Conflict, on so many levels, can bring out the worst in all of us. It often evokes irrational and dramatic responses that leaves us asking questions like: "How did we get to this point" and "What do we do now that this conflict exists?" Until now, many church leaders have not had the formal training or a set of tools to recognize, diagnose and effectively deal with dysfunctional conflict in the church.

In *Navigating Conflict,* the authors use their collective education, experience and expertise to provide insights and tools to help us work through our own humanity.

Safe, high-trust relationships don't happen by accident. They take work, effort and intentionality. If you are willing to put in the time and effort, you will find you can improve the quality of all the lives you touch along the way.

I am more than confident; this book will help you and your church navigate conflict more effectively!

Randy Mayes
CEO, DRYVE Leadership Group
Springfield, Missouri

Introduction

By this all people will know that you are my disciples, if you have love for one another. John 13:35

The two men were toe-to-toe, eyeball-to-eyeball, with their fists clenched as they stood on the elaborate production set. Their voices were raised, their faces red and any second one of them was going to punch the other one in front of the crowd of nearly 2,000 people.

While trying to calmly separate the two angry men, it was pointed out to them where they were standing. Ironically, they were having this argument in front of the tomb of Jesus! The very place where the Prince of Peace would soon triumphantly walk out after defeating death, these good men were ready to kill each other!

What was the argument all about anyway? Sin? A theological difference? A personal disagreement over something self-centered? None of the above, the argument was over the air conditioning and how it would impact the smoke on the stage during the Resurrection scene!

Both men loved the Lord and were hard working, faithful servants in the church. How could they get to the place where they were ready to push or hit each other? How could they miss the importance of where they were standing? How could this disagreement be settled in a mutually agreeable fashion? We hope to provide answers in the pages that follow...by the way, the conflict was settled peaceably, and the special effect was stunning!

Conflict among God's people is nothing new. Cain resolved his conflict with Able through murder (Gen 4:3-8). The herdsmen of Gerar quarreled with Isaac and his family (Gen 26:6-33). Moses experienced the pain and frustration of leading less than enthusiastic followers of the Lord (Numbers 14). This list could go on, but suffice to say, as long as humans are in the equation, God's people and His Church will continue to experience conflict.

This book is unique in that it is written from three very important perspectives that make up a more holistic view and approach to managing conflict. The perspectives of a pastor, a professor and a practitioner. Dr. Jeff Klick (pastor) is senior pastor of Hope Family Fellowship, a church he founded in 1993 after serving as a mega church administrator for eleven years. Dr. Rodney Harrison (professor) is a VP and professor at Midwestern Baptist Theological Seminary. Dr. Glenn Miller (practitioner) is the president and CEO of a company that has trained, consulted and worked the past 30 years with over 3,000 churches and ministries in accounting and administrative operations.

Paul's words to Corinth ring true today, "For God is not a God of confusion but of peace." (1Cor 14:33). A word to the wise; today, the word "peace" often invokes a passive picture. One showing an absence of civil disturbance, hostilities, or external strife. A better understanding of biblical peace is "to be complete" or "to be sound."[1]

Thus, a peacemaker is one who helps harness conflict and confusion in ways that will further the mission of the church or will mitigate conflict and confusion so that it does not hinder the church. Along the way, we hope to provide helpful, and healing insights for those who are weary and heavy laden from the fight.

This book is for those who love and care about the local church. It is a tool for pastors and church members who are committed to biblical integrity in addressing conflict and willing to examine their own motives and values. We recommend every reader approach these pages with a spirit of humility and a willingness to surrender our thoughts, actions and attitudes regarding issues of conflict to the Lordship of Jesus Christ.

Studies have shown many pastors leave the ministry primarily because of personal conflicts. Sticks and stones may break bones, but painful words and broken relationships have destroyed many churches and leaders, in spite of saying "words are not supposed to hurt us."

After completing our first book together – *Pastoral Helmsmanship: A Pastor's Guide to Church*

---

[1] Elwell, Walter A. "Entry for 'Peace'". "Evangelical Dictionary of Theology". 1997.

Administration, we have been delighted by the positive feedback received from our readers. Our goal was to produce a book that was practical, insightful, and actually useful in ministry.

Our second work in the Pastoral Series delved deeply into the overlooked, yet devastating problem of church fraud. *Confessions of a Church Felon* is opening eyes as to the reality of it and the solutions to end fraud. It is time for the Church to step up and embrace the need for financial integrity, and that tool will help any church of any size.

As we pondered what subject to tackle next, the obvious need of relational difficulty jumped out at us. Every church has people, and wherever two or more people gather, relationship issues will follow.

While there are many books and tools available dealing with relationship and conflict issues, we didn't find too many that address all three perspectives or that can serve as a practical guide. Our desire in writing this book is to be both.

It was my (Glenn) first fulltime church administration position. I was so excited to fulfill what I believe had been a calling since I was 12 years old. The leadership hired me to come in and "get the staff straightened out and get things moving." Perfect!

So, in one of my first staff meetings, I shared my vision for role clarity among the various staff positions, and a plan to also add accountability to the process. I proudly handed out ministry position descriptions along with a new, fresh off the press employee review system! Amongst the blank stares, I will never forget one of the associate pastor's response. He looked at the review form, tossed it back across the table to me and said in a very self-righteous voice "I work for God, I cannot possibly be evaluated by man!" Well, as you can imagine, I did not have a good response to that proclamation. Talk about creating conflict in the church! As you might imagine, he was soon after led by God to serve in another ministry.

Our Goal:

In the Scripture that opens this book, Jesus clearly stated that love for each other should be the identification of His followers. If anyone performs a Google search asking, "What is the Church of Jesus Christ known for?" love would not even appear. Ever. In fact, it is not until about seventy links into the search that anything positive even shows up! Sad.

> What is the Church known for?

The enemy of our souls has been very effective at discrediting the Church. Interpersonal conflict takes place at all levels within the Church. From pastors to boards, with and between staff, staff and members, and let us not forget between members of the congregation.

We do not have to read far into the Scriptures before we find relational issues. Once the primary relationship between God and His creation was broken because of sin, relational conflict and death were unleashed.

It is interesting how much of the Bible was written because humans simply could not get along with each other. Beginning with Adam blaming Eve in the Garden, and Cain killing Able afterward, relationship issues have dominated the human story.

After the primary relationship between God the Father and His first children was ruined by sin, every other relationship has had varying degrees of messiness. Marriage, parents and children, siblings, extended family, work, leisure and governmental relationships, have all been hindered with the unleashing of sin and death.

Moses was given the Law to help bring some order to a nation of slaves, with each pursuing whatever they wanted to do without basic kindness or regard for humans, animals or God.

The Historical books shed light on the results of rampant relational death with power-mad kings and tyrants, impacting thousands of lives.

The Poetical books share deep insights into everything from romance to sickness, from how to speak to when to be quiet.

We move into the Prophets and we see broken men with their kingdoms, and God's call back to a relationship with Himself. The Old Testament ends with a desire for healing of parental relationships, or the land itself will be struck with a curse.

Then, Life enters the human story. Christ is born, and everything begins to change. The answer to the age-old problem walks this earth, fulfills His mission to destroy sin and death, and ascends to the throne of the universe. The Good News has come!

But humans are still here. Even redeemed, born again, Spirit-filled men and women cannot seem to get along. Most of the New Testament letters were written to set straight what is crooked relationally.

From the tension between Jews and Gentiles to appealing to a slave owner to forgive and receive his slave back in good graces, the New Testament story is one of strained relationships...and the answer as to how to restore them to health!

It is helpful to be aware of these tensions as we read the Gospels, Epistles, and even Revelation. There is an answer to the human story with all our problems The answer is a Person. There is Jesus, the God-Man. Totally God and totally Man. There is the Gospel, the Glorious Good News of what God has accomplished to restore all relationships, beginning with the most important one - man to God.

We believe there are reasons behind dysfunctional conflict. We also believe there are constructive, practical solutions to minimize its negative effect on the church. We are not claiming this will be an easy process, but we do believe progress can be made with better understanding of the problem along with implementing some basic conflict management tools. That is our prayer and goal for this effort.

Although the book is best read as a whole, please feel free to jump to a particular section of interest. Each chapter will include a study guide that can be used individually or in a small group setting.

Knowing where we want to end up. Let us begin our journey together towards relational redemption.

Section I: Defining the Problem

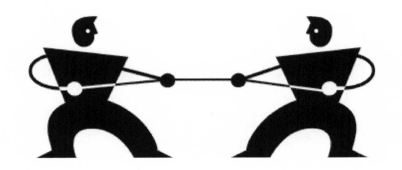

1. Are You Kidding Me?

And I confronted them and cursed them and beat some of them and pulled out their hair. Nehemiah 13:25 (a)

Moses was called to come up on the mountain to receive the written words by the hand of God. The scene must have been beyond description. The mountain covered in a cloud, thunder and lighting, and the air electric.

In fact, the seventy elders of Israel had just seen the pavement of sapphire stone under the feet of God Almighty.

As Moses is getting ready to ascend even higher on the mountain to receive the stone tablets, he reminds the elders in Exodus 24:14:

> And he said to the elders, "Wait here for us until we return to you. And behold, Aaron and Hur are with you. Whoever has a dispute, let him go to them."

"Come on man", as the famous sports quote states… Even in the physical presence of God Himself, Moses leaves instructions for how to deal with a dispute. Not much has changed in the Body of Christ since that day!

While we could spend hundreds of pages detailing conflict we have navigated, what follows are a small sampling of true stories to illustrate the wide-ranging scope of the problem.

Jeff:

The church had broken the 150-member barrier and was growing nicely. Home group meetings were the life blood of the relationship-oriented lifestyle of Her membership.

As young believers, we looked up to our small group leaders with all the admiration of a new puppy. We hung on their every word, and what they said, must be correct.

One night the discussion had a different flavor than normal, more hushed, dark and foreboding. Words like sin, split, and new direction were being bantered around. As the negativity grew, so did the momentum to do something about all this hidden sin. In fact, God demanded we must do something! Before we even knew what was really going on, the church split.

Men and women that used to be friends picked sides and spiritual death was unleashed in all directions. Accusations abounded, relationships tanked, and this new believer was in for a severe growth jolt.

When the dust settled everyone continued on, though many would never speak to each other again. Relational pain was high. The Lord had a lesson for my wife and I through this disaster.

Reading Proverbs 6:16-18 about six months later my eyes landed on these words:

> There are six things that the Lord hates, seven that are an abomination to him: haughty eyes, a lying tongue, and hands that shed innocent blood, a heart that devises wicked plans, feet that make haste to run to evil, a false witness who breathes out lies, and one who sows discord among brothers.

The Lord spoke very clearly to my heart that I had accomplished five out of the seven! Heartbroken, I broke down and wept. After discussing these matters with my wife, we went back to everyone we had spoken with to attempt to make things right. Most just laughed at us.

We met with the pastor and asked for forgiveness. He invited us to do the same the following Sunday morning. While embarrassed, we felt compelled to do so. God was doing a deep work in our hearts. We received forgiveness from the Lord and the pastor, for which we were very grateful.

What we did not or could not have possibly known was that same pastor would end up working on a staff with me nearly 20 years later. God had prepared the way because I was part of the executive team that provided oversight for that pastor two decades later. Can you imagine if we had not worked out our differences all those years earlier? Neither can I!

There are several lessons to learn from this experience of pain.

- God is redemptive.
- God knows the future.

- God loves humility.
- God hates sin so much He sent His Son to pay the price for it.
- Conflict is almost inevitable when humans are involved, but God is still able to redeem it for His glory.

Glenn:

Late in my dad's 40-year ministry career, he would sometimes call and ask me questions. I was honored to try to add something to his ministry. In his last church, over the final couple of years he was pastor, he shared about a growing rift between the treasurer and personnel committee.

For whatever reason, the treasurer wanted to assert more and more control over the church. Over a several year period, my dad would share with me many examples of the conflict that was ensuing. Finally, the personnel committee bought my dad a new office chair, and that was the final straw. The treasurer refused to pay the invoice, and the battle for control was on.

Sadly, it ended up splitting the church down the middle, and to this day, that ministry has never recovered. This sad reality has prompted many questions we are attempting to deal with:

- What was the real conflict?
- What was really going on?
- Could it have been avoided?
- Could it have been mitigated or even resolved without splitting the church?

I also once served on a large church staff where, frankly, the associate pastors and other ministry leaders did not always get along very well. The church was in an unprecedented period of growth, finances were strong, new buildings were going up, ministry was vibrant, and life was good, sort of.

Over the years, the team fell prey to jealousy, territorialism, greed, selfishness and power struggles. What? In a church? In a fast-growing vibrant church? Sadly, yes. During some contentious staff and leadership board meetings I would sit back and think to myself and hum the song in my head "...they will know we are Christians by our love, by our love, yes they'll know we are Christians by our love."

Eventually, over a period of years, those ungodly roots took hold to the point of staff turnover, and an eventual unprecedented mass firing. The church ended up splitting and those who stayed endured a long period of sickness and eventual church death. It was a strong and vibrant church of over 1,200 people. Today it no longer exists.

Again, questions circle in my mind:

- Did this have to happen?
- Was it preventable?
- Could something, anything have been done?
- Could things have turned out differently?

Rodney:
The 2:00 PM Meeting

At the conclusion of the Sunday morning service, our church plant's deacon asked my wife and I to "drop by the house around 2:00 pm for coffee." What was unknown to us was the rest of the church leaders and spouses had been invited to his house at 1:00 pm. When we arrived, the stage was set for a major confrontation.

For 40 minutes, the deacon and another leader shared their opinions about the direction of the church and my ability to effectively lead. The deacon's wife criticized my wife's competence as a mother and Proverbs 31 wife.

The issues raised were new to me but had been smoldering for months. There was frustration over a young camp transportation issue the previous summer and our church's participation in an upcoming community service.

Emotions ran high and tempers started to flare. I am pretty sure the only ones delighting in these deliberations were the devil and his demons. That afternoon I drafted a letter of resignation. Following the evening service, I asked our deacon to meet me for breakfast.

> Tell me your story.

After coffee was served, I asked our deacon to tell me his story. Surprised at the question, he hesitated, so I reiterated the question, "Tell me your story...where did you grow up, how did you come to know Christ?"

He proceeded to share his upbringing, attending church from his earliest memory, responding to the Gospel during a revival. He continued to share the story of a vibrant college ministry, seeing many come to faith in Jesus Christ, and after college, enrolling in seminary..." "Hold it! You went to seminary? Why?"

He proceeded to share what was, in essence, a call and initial response to ministry, which was forsaken due to hardship. As a result, over the years he regularly assumed roles in the church that allowed him to illegitimately assert pastoral leadership, as had occurred the previous day.

Since that time, I have documented several cases where the root of conflict arose from members called to vocational ministry, but who rejected or forsook the call. Could this be a source of conflict we overlook?

The Church Willing to Die over a Pulpit:

The previous pastor had attended a popular pastor's conference and was filled with ideas that would help turn the church around. Some of the changes were readily embraced, such as more contemporary music supplementing traditional hymns, and a renewed focus on biblical exposition and careful observance of church ordinances.

However, the removal of the pulpit (which was built by the namesake of the state mission offering) was too much. This monstrosity of a pulpit was about 7' in diameter. One has to walk into it to preach, and once inside, movement was limited.

The pastor was forced to resign over this conflict, and I was next in line to serve this historic church. In the year prior to the pastor's resignation, the church has declined from 120 to 40 in average attendance. The fiscal challenges of maintaining a facility designed for 500 worshippers is easy to imagine.

On my first Sunday, the massive pulpit had been restored to its "rightful place" on the platform behind the table used for serving the Lord's Supper. Since this pulpit was at the center of the conflict, I thought it would be good to know its history.

The builder was the first full-time pastor of the church. He was responsible for leading the church during a time of exceptional growth in the 1940's and led in the effort that resulted in the current campus and buildings.

The wood he used to build the pulpit was from the original church building. Two members this pastor had baptized in the 1940's were still active members, and among another group of remaining members were those whose parents had been evangelized and baptized by him. For these members the pulpit was symbolic of days of evangelistic fervency and growth.

The potential for an irreparable church split over the pulpit was high. The issue had already cost one pastor his position, and passions among pro-pulpit majority were intense. So, how was the issue resolved?

In this case, understanding the sources of the division (nostalgia, symbolic connections), much prayer for wisdom and a willingness to keep the matter in perspective in light of personal vs. Kingdom agendas would inform the solution.

After 12 months, the pulpit became the centerpiece of a heritage display consisting of the pulpit, the pastor's Bible and photos from the first two decades of the church's history. These artifacts attested to the church's past while inviting all who entered to become a part of the church's present.

Whether your conflict is a matter of clear biblical mandate or falls into the category of traditions, it is imperative to understand the potential for irreparable harm poorly managed conflict can inflict upon the membership and mission of the church.

We all want to believe there is a better way, there has to be. Perhaps a better understanding of the source of division and strife will be helpful as we continue our journey together in discovering how to walk through conflict in a redemptive fashion.

We will provide discussion questions at the end of each subsequent chapter to help you delve deeper into the material covered. Writing out answers or perhaps using them with a small group of others will help cement the content into your thinking and planning.

We are pretty sure by now you have come across at least one example or more you can relate to. We hope you are also asking the same questions we are:

- Is this type of destructive conflict inevitable?
- Does it have to be this way?
- When caught in the middle of a conflict, is there any way to navigate forward in a positive manner for the greater good?
- Or better yet, how can we promote healthy, constructive conflict and avoid destructive conflict all together?

2. The Sources of Division

What causes quarrels and what causes fights among you?
Is it not this, that your passions are at war within you?
James 4:1

Division is defined as the splitting of one or more things into multiple parts. Or, perhaps a math term is more appropriate for our thinking. Division results when we attempt to find a common denominator in order to get to the root. Four divided by two equals two.

James gets right to the root issue with his penetrating statement - *your passions are at war with you.* Ouch. We will explore additional causes of division later. For now, we must realize that at the bottom of many battles are sin, pride, and unfilled desires of the parties involved.

Most of us are immature and often act more like children than adults. We want what we want when we want it and we let everyone know how upset we are when we do not get it.

If you have been involved in working with people or have honestly done some self-evaluation, you know that sentence is true, even though painful. Very few of us are mature enough to allow others to get their own way at the expense of ours.

Think back over your most recent conflict regardless of who is involved and see if there is not an element of selfishness involved. Perhaps it can only be seen in the other party, but it is there on both sides of the conflict. We want what we want. We believe we are right in wanting it, and we will often fight more than we should, to get it. Not always, but certainly more than we should.

Even the most mature believer is less than perfect. There is a battle that rages within our hearts and minds and often that war escapes through our mouths. We hold our opinions as facts and very few people will continue to hold to a view they know to be in error. Therefore, we must be correct, and we must move everyone else to the right point of view – ours.

While we would probably all agree we should be seeking God's point of view, and the furthering of His Kingdom, we also believe we have the correct view of how that should be accomplished and everyone else is in varying states of error.

If everyone simply could look at each situation the way we do, then all would be well. That view may work for a period in a totalitarian system; it will not work in a family, church or on a leadership team.

In the verse under the chapter heading, James goes further regarding inward reflection by saying within each of us there is a war taking place. Our passions are driving us towards self and not towards God or love of others. If we are to change that outcome, we must learn to deal with the root problem.

Resolution vs. Suppression:

Major sources of conflict include: personality, process and values. Personality conflicts arise when our personal preferences are challenged or attacked.

The next chapter will go deeper into dealing with differing personality types, suffice to say, personality conflicts are a principal source of division and are often relationally driven.

Process conflicts are those that involve heart-felt differences of opinion or interpretation. Examples of process conflicts include church governance, and implementation of policies and staff reviews processes. Process, or task conflicts are often more objective in nature.

Value conflicts are ideologically driven and arise from differences in core beliefs. Examples may include budget expenditures for missions, the role of the church and staff in educating children and how the church recognizes special seasons, such as Christmas.

Let us start by exploring how something all Christians agree is essential to a healthy church. Prayer. The fact we all have personality preferences means that even prayer has the potential to lead to conflict. Using the learning styles identified by Marlene LeFever (Imaginative, Analytical, Common Sense and Dynamic) one recognizes each learning style has different preferences and approaches to prayer and worship, as noted in the following chart. [2]

Imaginative Learners	Analytical Learners
"Feel It and See It"	"Think and Plan"
Enjoys participating in a small, intimate prayer group	Enjoys theological and spiritual reading
Likes story-telling in sermons	Wants logical, challenging, 3-point sermons
Enjoys singing as a form of prayer	Engages in private prayer and spiritual journaling
Employs guided imagery in prayer	Enjoys opportunities for in-depth reflection on one's faith and life
Benefits from the use of symbols in worship and prayer	Develops a plan for spiritual growth
Common Sense Learners	**Dynamic Learners**
"Think and Act"	"Feel It and Do It"
After learning about new prayer forms, experiments with them	Likes new approaches to prayer and worship
Wants sermons with practical applications to daily life	Open to spontaneous prayer
Keeps an intercessory prayer list and uses it daily	Prefers active involvement in worship
Sees life activities as a form of prayer	Engages in prayer and worship with others in a group
	Participates easily in new worship and prayer rituals

Using this chart, one observes group prayer motivates the dynamic learners, whereas the analytical learner would prefer not to be forced into group prayer.

Imaginative learners embrace guided imagery in prayer, whereas the common-sense learner preference sees life activities as a form of prayer and would prefer a prayer list over public prayer requests.

These personality preferences extend to other aspects of church life but illustrate how personality preferences can easily give birth to conflict.

---

[2] Marlene LeFever, Learning Styles: Reaching Everyone God Gave You to Teach (Colorado Springs, CO, David C. Cook Publishing, 1995), 240.

Process (or task) conflict involves differences based on work details and goals. In many ways this is an easier type of conflict to resolve, as it responds well to communication of purpose and team dialogue. Process conflict that is not addressed can quickly devolve into personality conflict.

As would be expected, the earlier the process or task conflict is addressed, the greater the likelihood resolution.

In Exodus 18, Jethro, Moses' father-in-law, identifies a process conflict in the making. The process of hearing disputes, if left unresolved, had the potential for severe damage. Jethro observed, "people stand around you from morning till evening." My frustration over standing for 90 minutes at the DMV is bad enough, imagine the wait lasting from sunrise to sunset.

The key to Jethro's observation is he also included a solution. Pointing out his son-in-law's fault without a solution would have been unwise. In the same way, when addressing process conflicts in the church, providing a biblical response is always helpful.

For example, in the first chapter, I (Rodney) shared the account of a church whose leadership dismissed a pastor over the removal of a pulpit. The issue was the process of change.

As tempting as it is to place the blame upon church leadership, I see several parallels to Genesis 18. First, like Moses, the pastor was leading unilaterally. The church was open to change (as I experienced during my season of ministry with them). However, they wanted and needed to be a part of the process. It is likely the pastor questioned whether the people could be trusted.

Second, the people were standing around doing nothing. It has been said, "idleness is the devil's workshop." When I arrived, I discovered a congregation that had done little in the way of prayer, evangelism, ministry, outreach and fellowship. Unlike Moses, the former pastor did not have a Jethro. At least one neighboring pastor pointed out the "error of his way" regarding his leadership related to change, but none provided a clear solution.

Values can stem from conviction and traditions. Consider the fact that most Christians, when asked to pray, bow their head and close their eyes. Nowhere in Scripture will one find the bended head and closed eyes as prescriptive of effective prayer. However, I have seen many a child scolded for praying with eyes open or failing to bow their head. How the parents or Sunday School teacher knew this is still a mystery, but I digress.

Personal or congregational values can lead to disagreements. In the chart below, the categories are non-theological in the sense biblically orthodox churches globally can be found embracing each extreme of the continuum.

General Mood

Celebrative .... Solemn

Worship Planning

None .... Detail

Variety in the Worship Service

Little .... Much

Use of Technology

Low .... High

Music Style

Traditional .... Contemporary

Preaching Focus

Revelation .... Relevance

Response to Invitation

Private .... Public

Formality

Liturgical .... Informal

Use of the Arts & Drama

Low .... High

Visitors Recognized Publicly

Like .... Dislike

Recognizing that some values we hold close, such as the formality of worship and worship styles will help in understanding how conflicts can arise. This awareness is futile if individuals (or the church) are unwilling to address these issues. Unchecked, the sparks of minor personality, process or value conflicts can become full-fledged infernos. In his blog, Chuck Lawless identifies the following 10 conditions that allow conflict to escalate.[3]

1. **The church is made up of sinners.** This is the case, of course, and that fact won't change. Sinful people are naturally selfish and divisive. Sanctification sometimes takes a while to correct these tendencies.

2. **Members care about something.** This "condition" might seem strange, so hear my point. Some conflict in the church heats up in direct proportion to how much people care about some issue in the church. Their care may be misdirected, and their sense of ownership may be problematic – but they fight for something precisely because they care about it that much.

3. **The church has no "up front" relational expectations.** The churches I know that deal well with conflict are usually those who teach how to deal with relational conflict *as early as their membership class.* The church that ignores these potential issues invites problems.

4. **Nobody's praying for unity.** Jesus prayed this way in John 17:21 – "May they all be one, as You, Father, are in Me and I am in You. May they also be one in Us, so the world may believe You sent Me." If Jesus prayed that prayer for His followers, we, too, should be praying for this unity.

5. **Church leaders have not taught biblical principles for conflict resolution.** Matthew 18:15-20 is a starting point. Putting others before self (Phil. 2:3) obviously matters. Believers who don't know what

---

[3] http://chucklawless.com/2015/08/10-reasons-conflict-escalates-in-the-church/

the Bible teaches about reconciliation will follow
the ways of the world – and the way of the world is
often, "I want to win."

6. **Leaders do not address legitimate concerns.** At
   times, the concerns church members raise are
   legitimate. When church leaders blatantly ignore
   those concerns, nonchalantly hear them, or
   superficially address them, the conflict is not
   resolved. Its resolution is only delayed.

7. **Conflict is not separated from emotion.** I think, for
   example, of battles over worship styles. These
   preferences are so connected with emotions that it's
   often difficult to separate the two. Conflict
   escalates because emotions heat up.

8. **People operate in secret.** You know the scenarios.
   Anonymous complaints. Unsigned letters. Behind
   the scenes meetings. Opposition rallies cloaked as
   "prayer meetings." It is all secretive – and it is
   often demonic.

9. **People listen to gossip.** Once conflict begins, rumor
   and innuendo often fuel it. Those who spread the
   rumors are acting in sin, but so are those folks who
   stoke the coals by listening. If anyone listens, the
   fire spreads.

10. **Nobody carries out church discipline.** It would be
    ideal if all conflict were resolved before discipline
    became necessary. The Bible, though, assumes that
    churches will take the necessary steps to deal with
    troublesome members. If the church doesn't do so
    (or, if they do so, but in an unbiblical or
    uncharitable way), they prolong the conflict.

Identifying the source of conflict—whether personality,
process or values, is not always an easy task. It is also
only a first step. Unless members are willing to address
the conflict, the devil wins.

The elephants in the room:

Over the course of nearly four decades, I (Rodney) have reviewed hundreds of church constitutions and by-laws submitted by students as a class assignment. Tragically, some never address matters of conflict and discipline. Those that do seldom go beyond Matthew 18:15-19, overlooking the backdrop of the matter, humility (18:1-4) and inserting an inappropriate break between verses 14 and 15.

The opposite of humility is not pride, as many assume, but selfishness. Humility is about others. Selfishness is about me. Humility is a Kingdom mindset. Selfishness seeks personal victories. A lack of humility can manifest itself in personality, process and value conflicts. Take time to read all of Matthew 18 before moving on to the reflection questions at the end of this section.

At the heart of much conflict is the feeling someone (often oneself) is not being treated fairly. It is ironic many in the church feel they have a right to fairer treatment than Jesus received.

The psalmist wrote, "He guides the humble in what is right and teaches them His way." (Psalm 25:9). Humility and teachablity go hand in hand. Thus, the first elephant in the room of conflict is a lack of humility.

The second elephant in the room of conflict is a lack of forgiveness. Forgiveness is not always easy, but it is always possible. God commands us to forgive. Jesus taught, "Whenever you stand praying, forgive, if you have anything against anyone, so that your Father who is in heaven will also forgive you your transgressions." (Mark 11:25)

In 2002 a trusted church leader sexually abused our daughter. I recall the emotions and visceral feelings that sought to overwhelm my actions. And yet, at that very moment I recalled the words of Jesus on the cross, "Father, forgive them, for they do not know what they are doing."

Shortly afterwards, my daughter and I prayed not only for the ability to forgive the perpetrator, but that the Lord would grant us the grace to love him as well. The decision to forgive (and love) made all the difference. To be clear, the crime was reported, and the perpetrator held accountable for his action. Forgiveness does not change the past, rather, it gives focus to the future.

Are the elephants of selfishness and unforgiveness present in the conflict you are experiencing? We cannot force others to forgive—but we can, and must, forgive even their "unforgiveness." We cannot cause another to humble themselves before God or others, but we can submit our thoughts, actions and attitudes of selfishness into the arms of our loving Father.

Before moving on perhaps it would be wise and helpful to stop and ask the Lord about your own heart and emotions. Do either of these elephants need to be dealt with in your life?

Discussion/application questions:

1) Discuss issues of conflict you have seen or heard in previous ministry settings without assigning blame.
2) What are the implications, if any, of the transition between Matthew 18:14 and 18:15? (You did take the time to read Matthew 18, right?)
3) What traditions or values do you hold to that might not be based in Scripture?
4) Using the values continuum, what are some potential areas of disagreement between the membership and senior leadership and between the church and potential prospects?
5) For now, make a list of all real or perceived issues for future diagnosis and discussion.

3. Dealing with Differing Personality Types

But grace was given to each one of us according to the measure of Christ's gift. Ephesians 4:7

Why can't we all get along? Why can't everyone see things as clearly as I do? Why do some people seem to always need to be the center of attention and others hide in the background? Why are some people detailed oriented and others can't seem to ever get the facts right? Did God make a mistake?

It is almost a universal principle that opposites attract. Why is that? Ask just about any married couple and they will reply they married someone exactly opposite of them. The detail person married the big picture one. The organized person married the disorganized. Why? Is it part of some cosmic plan, or simply just the way it is?

While we may never know all the reasons for those choices, we do know inwardly we are attracted to someone different than us simply because of that difference. It's as if we know we need something beyond our self. God made us each in our own unique style for a reason. We need each other. We are not all there is, and we do not have all the answers. Here is an old saying to ponder:

"If two people are exactly alike one of them is not necessary."

Back in the 1960's, there was a Twilight Zone episode that explored this concept. The main character was frustrated with all the differences between people. He bemoaned that if everyone was just like him life would be perfect. Because it was TV and the Twilight Zone, this man received his wish. He awoke the next day and everyone he met was just like him. As all of us know, it took about three minutes for this dream of sameness to turn into a nightmare.

God, the ultimate Creative Genius, has declared we all will be different. We all think differently, are emotionally wired uniquely and reflect an aspect of His nature. No two people are exactly alike including identical twins. You may have known twins, and it does not take long before they don't even look alike to you, let alone act and think alike. God is creative and He values difference - so should we.

Personality Profile Tools:

With all the free resources available today on the Internet, I (Glenn) am amazed at the number of students at the bachelor and master levels that I teach at seminary, who have not discovered their unique personality profile. But how does knowing your personality style and preferences help navigate conflict?

For many years I have used a progression of terms to describe how we can learn to work together more effectively. The progression looks like this[4]:

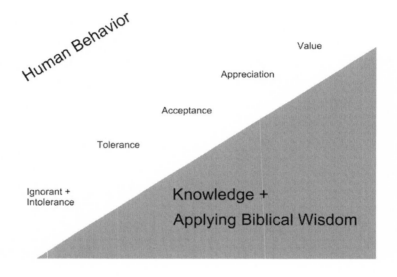

When we are ignorant and intolerant, we have no hope of working well together. When we add some knowledge and Biblical wisdom, we hopefully begin to move forward past just tolerating people. As we learn about ourselves and others, we begin to recognize and hopefully accept God's

---

[4] Graph of human behavior = Miller Management Systems, LLC, "Discovering, Valuing and Working With Different Personality Styles" Page 6, July 2018

design. Then we can move toward truly appreciating each other which then ultimately can lead to genuinely valuing each other. When we truly value each other as God intends us to, then we can work with healthy conflict and keep it from sinking into dysfunctional conflict.

We typically recommend the use of some form of the DiSC behavioral profile. It comes in many forms and can be found on the Internet for free. Some firms offer a more in-depth analysis but at a cost.

The reason we prefer DiSC is because it is consumable by the average person. The four-quadrant analysis is easy to comprehend and provides more in-depth information with the addition of each person's "classic profile" if desired. If we could begin to understand the concept of the four quadrants, it would be of great value to our churches.

The four primary styles come with four labels. Note these are just labels, not meant to be the end all descriptor of an individual. It breaks down as follows:

D = Dominant style

The textbook description for a "D" style personality is:

"Emphasis is on shaping the environment by overcoming opposition to accomplish results."

In our firm, we like to use the concept of a canoe trip in describing the four types of canoers in hopes of making it a bit easier to remember and frankly add a bit of humor to the learning process.

We like to affectionately refer to these folks as the "**Mad Paddlers**." They can be found on the canoe trip saying things like:

- "Let's go! We've wasted enough time talking, get in the canoe!"

- "Come on, stroke, stroke, stroke, we can beat the other canoes there!"

- "We can take those rapids! Hang on!"

- "Yes, we lost one small child and a dog, but we were the first ones back to base camp!"

I think you get the idea.

The next quadrant represents the "I" style.

I = Influencer style

The textbook defines these folks as:

"Emphasis is on shaping the environment by influencing or persuading others."

Our canoe trip metaphor has these folks labeled as "**Splashers**" and saying things like:

- "Can we stop here and play in the water a while?"

- "Hey look, a place to sit and talk!"

- "Don't you just love the scenery, the beauty, the leisure of it all?"

- "Just being here with you all makes the snakes, bugs and canned Spam all worth it!"

Group hug anyone?

S = Steadiness style

The textbook characterizes these folks as:

"Emphasis is on cooperating with others to carry out the task"

In our scenario, we refer to them as "**Life Preservers**" and you can hear them say things like:

- "Would everyone be happier if we stopped and ate lunch together?"

- "Would anyone like my .8 portion of a soda?"

- "Straying off course for a small adventure? Ummmm, I'd prefer to keep to the plan, if that is alright with everyone else."

- "I know this is a long and difficult journey, I feel your pain, literally!"

In one workshop we ask participants to self-describe their style and the "S" style group said, "We are the ones most like Jesus!" ☺

C = Conscientious style

The textbook definition for this style is

"Emphasis is on working conscientiously within existing circumstances to ensure quality and accuracy"

We call these wonderful folks, **"The Mappers"**. They can be heard saying:

- "Ok, I just want to review our inventory of supplies one last time before we leave."

- "According to my calculations, we should pass a large oak tree with an eagles' nest 24 feet 3 inches up from the first Y branch left of the large granite rock just around the next bend in approximately 4.32 minutes.......... this is so exciting!"

- "Ok, there are exactly 1.8 cans of soda for everyone on the trip, so enjoy!"

- "If we were all rowing with our paddles at the same depth as the manual called for, we could use approximately 16% less energy and arrive at our destination 12.2% early!"

I think we all know who our mappers are in our respective groups.

So obviously one point here is people are definitely different. God made us this way for a purpose, so we would need each other or as a display of His sense of humor, or perhaps both.

But now how does this tie to managing conflict more effectively? Remember the graphic display earlier, knowledge can and should lead to tolerance, which should then give way to acceptance and hopefully lead to appreciation and value. That in and of itself would be a major step forward for most of us. But there is more to understand here.

One key to mastering conflict between differing personality styles is understanding the "**why**" behind the "**what**"! Ok, so a "D" has a pushy style, so what? And, the "I" cares about people more than I do, who cares?

Better relational understanding will develop from thinking about the four overarching tendencies that appear in boxes on top and on the sides of the diagram below.

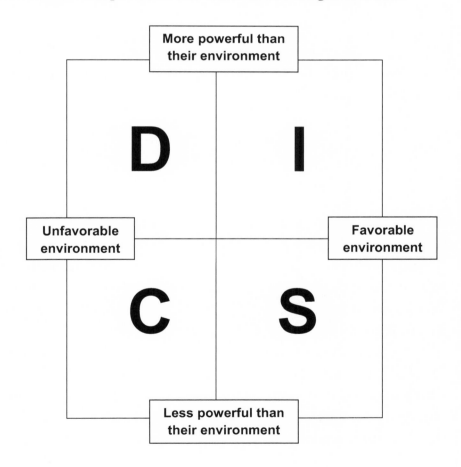

On top, the Ds and Is inherently share the belief they are more powerful than their environment. It doesn't matter if it is true or false, that is what they firmly believe and as such, it significantly influences their behavior.

On the left, Ds and Cs share a common belief that in general, the environment is unfavorable, and therefore they must proceed with caution and control, force if necessary.

To the right, the Is and Ss share a more optimistic view of the environment and that it is generally favorable, so chill out!

And on the bottom, the Cs and Ss share the belief in general, they are less powerful than their environment, and thus appear at times to be passive in their approach because they don't believe they can change their environment to any great degree. So why try?

So, how is this knowledge helpful? In one of my (Glenn) church administration roles, the church had nearly a million dollars in reserves. The buildings were in disrepair, the parking lots needed work and even from a distance, the property looked like it need attention. The computer systems were outdated, and the software was obsolete. Tables and chairs in many classrooms were worn out or worse, broken.

Despite the obvious needs, you could hear leadership say regularly "We have money in reserve for a rainy day! You never know when you might need those reserves. We have been good stewards and saved God's money." (I often wanted to ask them about the parable of the talents that was left to the three servants to care for and invest.)

The leadership mantra they claimed to hold near and dear to their heart was "We believe in excellence in ministry!" Really? It didn't look like it from where I stood.

How could any leadership group claim excellence in ministry and not use some of the reserves to bring the operation up to par? The answer is quite simple, the group was made up of four "Cs and one "D". That's how!

This Godly group of leaders cared deeply for the church and its wellbeing in the only way they knew how to, with their God given insights and leanings. The only problem is they camped primarily in one quadrant of insight! They only had 25% of the picture.

I knew I was in for some conflict when I asked for $600k of reserves to bring the operation up to standards. Through careful education and planning, we got it done. When I left that church 5 years later, we had a beautifully remodeled campus inside and out, and had fully restored the $600k spent!

Keys to understanding the various personality types thinking and motivations, the "why" behind the "what"[5]:

"D" The Mad Paddler:

When the environment is perceived as unfavorable and the person feels more powerful than the environment, he or she will act to change, fix or control the situation.

---

[5] Definitions starting with Mad Paddler = Miller Management Systems, LLC ""Discovering, Valuing and Working with Different Personality Styles" Page 8, July 2018

"I" The Splasher:

When the environment is perceived as favorable and the person feels more powerful than the environment, they will act to persuade others to their point of view.

"C" The Mapper:

When the environment is perceived as unfavorable and the person feels less powerful than the environment, they will respond by setting clear rules within the situation and work hard to follow them.

"S" The Life Preserver:

When the environment is perceived as favorable and the person feels less powerful than the environment, they will work to support the situation as it is and support others as well.

Learning and understanding these nuances will not come quickly or easily, but they are worth repeatedly reviewing, discussing and integrating into training for managers and leaders at all levels.

So, here are some tips to leveraging your new found understanding of personality styles:

1. Make sure your ministry, pastoral, and leadership teams, or any other team or committee has at least 3 out of the 4 quadrants represented for more balanced input and processing.

2. How do you know for sure how balanced or unbalanced your team is? Don't guess! Do an

assessment, preferably the DiSC and find out for sure. I never work with a leadership team until or unless I know who is on the team.

3. Teach the depth of each style, have fun with the positives and negatives each style brings to the table. Take the time to get to know one another, gain in wisdom and understanding that will hopefully lead to greater respect and value for each other. That alone should reduce dysfunctional conflict.

4. When conflict happens, understand better where each of you is coming from. Exchange ideas based on the understanding you have a limited view of the situation, just from your quadrant.

5. Listen, and then listen some more. Gain understanding.

Personality styles are God given. They can either work against us (dysfunctional conflict) or they can be used to generate healthy, functional, productive conflict.

Discussion/Application questions:

After taking a DiSC assessment, sit down with your group, team, or family and discuss the key points of this chapter.

1) Did God *really* make us all this different? Why?
2) Which style is the best for ministry effectiveness? (trick question meant to stir relevant debate)
3) Which style was Jesus? (Again, trick question, Jesus was the perfect balance of all four, we obviously are not, and therefor need each other!)
4) Is our staff and/or leadership group leaning heavily toward one quadrant? If so, is that a present or potential issue?
5) How does our group, staff or leadership team reflect the makeup of our congregation?
6) Do we really need four quadrant balances on our team? If so, how do we achieve it?
7) If we take a more balanced approach, what might be the benefits?

4. Hotbeds for Conflict

*What I mean is that each one of you says, "I follow Paul,"
or "I follow Apollos," or "I follow Cephas," or "I follow
Christ." I Corinthians 1:12*

Wherever two or three are gathered a possible conflict
will follow. In the church, it seems like there are so many
ways to get into a fight.

When we (Jeff) moved to a small town in the late 1970's
we found a church related to the one that was in the city
we just left. We were overjoyed! This growing church had
just moved into a new facility and excitement was high.
The church was growing numerically and was becoming
well-known in the small community.

After a month or two, the pastor declared the elders
were no longer elders and the elders threatened to remove
the pastor physically from the pulpit if he showed up on

Wednesday evening. The church split, many in the town mocked and multiple lessons were never learned.

In our church world, conflict potential abounds, because most of those involved have deep seeded beliefs regarding their church.

Here is a sampling of potential conflicts any gathering can fall into. Some we will develop later in more detail. This list is not given to depress us, but to make us aware.

- Vision
- Worship
- Staffing
- Pastor vs. Elders or Deacons or Board
- Power struggles
- Financial issues
- Disgruntled volunteers
- Hurt feelings due to the pastor's message
- Hurt feelings for being overlooked
- Hurt feelings in general
- Feeling judged or criticized
- Seating
- Missions giving
- Youth ministry style
- Children's ministry
- Parking
- Buildings
- Church discipline
- Lack of love, peace, joy, _____
- Not being fed, cared for, involved, _____

If we add to the above list any theological disagreements, we could expand it greatly. For example:

- Calvinist vs. Armenian
- Charismatic vs. Cessation
- End Times Choices - Pick one (or several)
- Bible Translations
- Denominational preference or flavor
- Traditional vs. contemporary worship
- Pro-Seminary or against academics
- Formal dress vs. casual
- Baptism rituals
- Communion
- Seeker friendly, evangelism, discipleship or some other service style
- Drama, dance, use of the arts
- _____

The list of potential conflicts is almost endless. Just as the conflicts of our age differ from those of the first century (such as eating meat sacrificed to idols, questions of circumcision and women's hair coverings), each generation will face new issues that potentially can lead to conflict.

What we want to do in this chapter is not bemoan the fact of conflict but raise the level of awareness and provide some tips and pointers of how to deal with the inevitable.

The fact there is conflict is in itself not evil, but often a reflection of passion. Sin can enter when we fail how to live in harmony with others holding differing views. When we care deeply about a point of view, preference or belief, we are often willing to defend it.

The problem is not with the underlying passion but the way we often tend to express our views. We find it difficult to accept the fact someone else might see something differently from us. Sometimes we feel threatened or judged if they do.

Good people often argue over small issues. In fact, many church splits and long-term relationships end over seemingly insignificant matters. Leadership teams choose camps, pastors provoke elders and deacons, and Christians split and divide. Why?

As we have already observed, Jesus said in John 13:35: *"By this all people will know that you are my disciples, if you have love for one another."*

Love of one another is our calling card to the lost and to each other. Yet, if we stopped a person on any street corner and asked them to describe the followers of Jesus, would "full of love" be their answer?

> Good people often argue over small issues.

Sadly, the Church is known more for fighting, division, strife, and seeking after money, than love. So, why the lack of love? Why is it that we do not love as we have been loved by Love Himself?

There are many reasons of course, including sin, selfishness, and pride. One issue is we tend to believe we are right about almost anything and everything. If someone disagrees with us, they *must* be wrong. We believe that our point of view is the correct one, for normal people do not hold on to opinions they know are in error. Therefore, if you disagree with me, you must be wrong.

This principle is true with our personal value system as well. We tend to evaluate everyone else by the plumb line of our standards. I, of course, am balanced and correct. You, therefore, are either right or left of me. You are either more liberal or legalistic based on my view, which is always correct.

We probably wouldn't say such things out loud, but if we stop and think about it, we do believe this way, for who would willingly hold to an opinion or view that they know is in error? It is very difficult for us to accept the fact others may see things differently and still be correct.

Many marriages, families, churches, and employments end due to not understanding there are many acceptable ways to think, act, and do the job. Demanding my way is right; therefore, your way must be wrong, will lead to tension and often division.

As illustrated in a previous chapter, no two people are exactly alike or one of them is not really needed! God created each of us to be unique expressions of His Image. Demanding everyone else conform to us and our way of thinking will lead to stress, strife, and broken relationships. There is more involved of course, but certainly not less. When we learn to value others as much as being right, we will make great strides in living the resurrected life

Perhaps you have had as many conversations about a theological point of view as I have. After hours of debate, the person says something along the lines of, "You just do not understand the issues involved." We had just spent hours debating the finer points of the topic and this is the conclusion offered as to why we do not agree. The option that we simply do not agree was never even considered, because if I understood what my opponent was saying, of course I would agree with them!

Many of us struggle to allow others to hold a differing point of view and that is tragic and usually divisive. The absence of this ability often not only leads to arguing and division, but the failure to arrive at much better decisions and conclusions. If we remain the sum total of correct information, we will always be limited.

Good people can honestly disagree with one another and remain friends and co-workers. Humility is required, and we would strongly argue it is possible, and we would add, necessary for the Kingdom.

There are many reasons for division, strife, and disagreement, and some we have detailed already – differing personalities and conflict styles, deeply held passions and our tendency to believe we are correct on all matters, therefore, everyone else is in varying degrees of error.

None of us is perfect and all of us have blind spots. God's Word is clear that we must learn how to walk in love towards others, and then those around us will take notice of our Gospel.

Given the sheer number of "hotbed" issues we face, how do we learn to walk in love, grace and unity one to another? We will share additional insights in later chapters, but for now, consider some of these choices covered in the following questions.

Discussion/Application Questions:

1) Can we learn to allow others to hold differing views by realizing we are not the sum of all truth and wisdom?

2) Is there any chance that we could be wrong or not entirely correct regarding an issue?

3) Can we learn to choose to overlook an offense? Is so, how do we walk it out? Proverbs 19:11 states "Good sense makes one slow to anger, and it is his glory to overlook an offense."

4) Can or will we allow time for people to grow, as we desire others to allow us time to mature?

5) Can we agree we are all in varying degrees of maturity and none of us are finished yet in the process?

6) Can we evaluate whether an issue is a sin topic or view, or simply a personal preference not clearly defined by Scriptural mandate?

7) Can we choose to walk in 1 Corinthians love towards one another by God's grace and empowerment?

5. Is All Conflict Bad?

For, in the first place, when you come together as a church, I hear that there are divisions among you. And I believe it in part, for there must be factions among you in order that those who are genuine among you may be recognized. I Corinthians 11:18-19

Having just examined why there is so much conflict, and discussing some of the hotbeds in which it breeds, we felt it would be helpful to look at the other side of the issue as well - is all conflict bad or unnecessary?

The short answer is, "no." Sometimes conflict arises from a lack of communication and if addressed, can be redemptive. In other cases, conflict forces both parties to examine their viewpoints and perhaps consider each other's valid, redemptive points.

Conflict can also reveal when a relationship is toxic and should be stopped. Perhaps leaders need to take a second look at their vision, mission, and positions or whether they can or should continue to support a vision, mission or position based on repeated dysfunctional conflict.

Conflict often reveals what is in our hearts that we have suppressed. We cannot deal with bad attitudes, sinful behaviors and misunderstandings when we remain unaware of them, conflict can force them out into the light, so they can be dealt with fully.

Conflict is often needed to bring restoration. In salvation, we needed to know we were at odds with our Creator due to our sin before we could receive the remedy of it.

While most of us love the peaceful times in our lives, if we are honest, it is during the storms we cry out to God and grow the most. There is nothing like a full blown, knock down battle to get to the root of our heart issues.

Implementing change can be very good to reinvigorate a struggling ministry, but this often takes place in the midst of great conflict. Is the conflict worth it? Absolutely.

In marriage, parenting, leadership, and membership, conflict can be redeeming, eye-opening, and life-changing. The result often depends on how we walk through it and if we are really seeking God's Kingdom and His will. Death to self is painful, but redemptive.

A wound of a friend is better than the kisses of an enemy, Proverbs 27:6 states, and yet, wounds typically only happen in the midst of a conflict. Perhaps we would be wiser to embrace a more Biblical mindset when considering conflict.

As Gregg Thompson, author of *The Master Coach* states,

"The word confrontation is usually defined as a conflict between people's beliefs and opinions. I prefer to define it as a courageous encounter with the truth – whatever that truth might be."[6]

A courageous encounter with the truth is an excellent thought to consider if conflict is good or bad.

Functional and Dysfunctional Conflict:

Let's define and examine the difference between "functional" and "dysfunctional" conflict. Since we are all familiar with dysfunctional conflict, we will begin there.

Merriam-Webster's on-line dictionary provides some insight to a comprehensive understanding of our terms:

Dysfunction: impaired functioning, abnormal or unhealthy interpersonal behavior or interaction within a group or family

Conflict: competitive or opposing action of incompatibles, antagonistic state or action (as of divergent ideas, interests, or persons) a *conflict* of principles, mental struggle resulting from incompatible or opposing needs, drives, wishes, or external or internal demands, the opposition of persons or forces that gives rise

---

[6] The Master Coach: Leading with Character, Building Connections, and Engaging in Extraordinary Conversations (Bluepoint Leadership Series) 2017

to the dramatic action in a drama or fiction (seems to apply in that many would say life is but a drama!)

So, if we combine and paraphrase just a bit, we might come up with a working definition that looks something like this:

The impaired, abnormal and unhealthy interpersonal behavior that creates an antagonistic state of unresolved conflicting ideas fueled by opposing needs, drives, and wishes that translate into internal or external demands giving rise to opposing persons taking dramatic actions.

Sound familiar? We probably can recognize this definition in many areas of our lives, with our children, spouses, friends, coworkers and of course, at church.

The "Christianized" definition for the Church:

The collision of spiritually immature and/or unhealthy selfish people who allow their personal wants and desires to supersede praying and seeking God's plan. They chose to force their opinions on others instead of working with others in community to discover God's best for His Church.

Please allow a short rabbit trail: I (Glenn) have heard many church leaders say over the years "Well, that's just how I am," referring to how argumentative and contentious they are. Well, presuming God made everyone, and the Bible speaks volumes about how we should act and how we should treat people, I think it is safe to assume that God did NOT make you that way. It is a choice, and perhaps it is time to make some new choices! Back to business.

So, what are the effects of dysfunctional conflict on relationships and the church?

Obvious effects include:

- Unnecessary tension in meetings creates stress for participants and limits the meeting's success.

- Limits forward progress on many major initiatives.

- A poor witness to unbelievers and community members.

- Creates an environment where people do not want to participate and might even lead to leaving the church.

- Sends a very poor message to potential new members.

- Potential good ideas are left in the rubble of dysfunction.

- Promotors of dysfunction end up controlling the outcomes which rarely move the ministry forward.

Less obvious effects include:

- It tends to silence good people with good ideas. Some people are wired where they cannot or will not deal with dysfunctional conflict and instead, stay silent or walk away.

- Sets a bad example for our children. Children pick up more bad habits of ours than we are willing to admit. This can impact generations to come!

- Grieves the heart of God and impacts His blessing on the ministry over the long hull. We sometimes wonder why things aren't going well in ministry, could it be God is not pleased with our behavior toward one another?

We should not be easily convinced that "Well, people are just people, we all have issues, stuff happens..." We can and should deal with dysfunctional conflict. If we do not know any better or do not have a better way, sometimes people just settle for the status quo.

Let's not do that, let's examine what functional or healthy conflict looks like.

The very term itself at first appears to be an oxymoron. The reason we feel that way is because we see so much dysfunctional conflict, it is hard to imagine what functional or healthy conflict even looks like. Let's return to Merriam-Webster[7] for some help.

Functional: connected with, or being a <u>function,</u> affecting physiological or psychological <u>function,</u> used to contribute to the development or maintenance of a

---

[7] Webster's online dictionary - http://www.learnersdictionary.com/

larger whole, designed or developed chiefly from the point of view of use, performing or able to perform a regular function

Conflict: competitive or opposing action of incompatibles, antagonistic state or action (as of divergent ideas, interests, or persons) a *conflict* of principles, mental struggle resulting from incompatible or opposing needs, drives, wishes, or external or internal demands, the opposition of persons or forces that gives rise to the dramatic action in a drama or fiction

If we once again combine and paraphrase to garner a workable definition, we offer:

Connecting with others physiologically and psychologically to contribute to the development or maintenance of something greater than ourselves. This allows for opposing views to be heard and considered and promotes working and laboring together to seek out the common good and to formulate a common understanding of the outcomes desired.

The "Christianized" definition for the Church might look something like:

The understanding that as God's children, each of us have spiritual, physiological and physical gifts to contribute to Kingdom work. As such, we need to treat people with respect, truly listen to them, and work together in seeking God's plan for the Church.

For greater clarity, let me illustrate. When I, (Glenn) attended Pastor Jeff's church, we came to a point in time where we needed a new facility because we had outgrown the existing facility. So off I went, as did others, to find the "right" building for the church. Unfortunately, we all had very different ideas about what was right!

After months of praying and searching, searching and praying, the choice came down to two ideas: purchase land and build a new facility custom designed to meet our specific needs (yeah!!, I even had some artist renderings and some wonderful acreage out in the country off of a major highway,) or buy an old Morton building that needed lots of updating that was in a not so great area of town. (boooo, clearly a bad idea). I guess you can kind of tell which idea I thought was the best plan, my plan of course!

Seeing the potential conflict coming, Pastor Jeff wisely sent the group off to pray for two weeks. His instruction was "Seek the Lord in prayer for what is God's plan for the church, not your plan." He also instructed us that he was not convinced this was about which plan we should follow, but rather about how we seek God and work together."

So off we went. When we came back together, I was amazed. God had laid on my heart that even though I was a genius and had done some great work, it was not God's plan for the church. Others shared their perspectives and we were in unity to purchase the Morton building.

> Unity commands a blessing.

Later, through God's mighty hand, we were able to buy that property at about 50% of the market value, and with the down payment from the old building sale and renting out a second building that came with the new property, the church never paid any additional money for their new facility! Ok, I guess God's plan was better than mine. A few years later the city came through and put in a beautiful new road in front of the church! God is good.

The Bible says. "Unity commands a blessing," in Psalm 133. Unity is an excellent goal and within unity a great deal of Kingdom work can be accomplished.

Unity does NOT mean cloning, compliant silence, peace at any cost or monolithic thinking. It does mean God working in and through us working together and there, commands the blessing of God!

The advantages of functional or healthy conflict?

- In seeks to include all of God's people, not just the extroverts.

- It seeks to allow all of God's people's to be heard, understood and vetted with respect.

- It tends to draw out all participants in a safe and healthy atmosphere.

- Sometimes partial, half-formed ideas, concepts and possibilities lead to better ideas.

- A great example to unbelievers and the community.

- A great model for our kids to follow.

- Once ideas, concerns and viewpoints are heard, it should allow for appropriate time to think, pray and get the mind of God. "It seemed good to us and the Holy Spirit."

- It should promote a healthy level of unity in the church to allow it to move forward.

What can we do to promote functional/healthy conflict in our boards, staffs and congregation?

1) Treat people with respect always, even when you disagree.

2) Listen AND hear what others are saying, especially when it is different from your perspective.

3) Seek to understand, not just being understood. Really try to understand the opposing view. You don't have to agree with it but acknowledging other's points and perspectives goes along way.

4) Invite a diverse group to the table to hear all sides, not just folks you agree with!

5) Allow for and even nurture half-formed concepts and possibilities. Dialog, dig deep. A finished idea seldom comes on the first try.

6) Pray and seek God's plan. Always provide meaningful times of prayer and devotions before meetings.

7) Take the necessary time for God to work with and through others, even if you are sure of the path.

8) Pray, pray and then pray some more. I think a good rule of thumb is "pray or pay!"

Let's not quickly assume all conflict is bad, unproductive or to be avoided. Let's instead show the world how to disagree with civility and care for each other in the process, and then "they will know we are Christians by our love!"

Discussion/application questions:

1) Describe examples of where you have seen functional conflict help a ministry make a godly choice.
2) What are some ways you can intentionally encourage functional conflict in your group, leadership, team or church?
3) How can you create a safe space in your ministry relationships for the benefits of functional conflict to positively impact your ministry?
4) How can you practice the "art of functional conflict?" and embed it is your organization's culture?

Section II: The Practical Side of Managing Conflict

6. Discovering Your Conflict Style

And when his disciples James and John saw it, they said, "Lord, do you want us to tell fire to come down from heaven and consume them?" Luke 9:54

Each of us is different and that is a good thing. Not only are we unique expressions of our Creator, we each bring a set of strengths, weaknesses, insights, and variables to every situation. This too is good.

We also each use a style as we walk through inevitable conflicts. What follows is an explanation of various styles of dealing with and walking through conflict. These are not broken into right and wrong, but simply explain what they are. The truth is all of us are a complex mixture of choices that sometimes change rapidly depending on the situation.

Like the DiSC profile that focuses on personality, the following set of insights deals with your unique conflict management style. None of these are exclusive and all of them are probably going to be used over the course of our life, but each of us has a primary style we default to more than the others and a secondary style we are comfortable using. Unfortunately, we tend to neglect the styles not of our preference, even when it might be the most prudent given the nature of the conflict.

These tools are insightful to help us know ourselves and others better. If we can accept the fact that not everyone is like us, nor needs to be, we will go far. As you examine these styles, you will probably find yourself saying, "That's me!" We must learn to understand our own preferred style before we can learn to fully appreciate others.

Jesus was the model of perfection and all of us are in various stages of imperfection. If Jesus took these type assessments, we assume He would hit dead center in all of them. Since none of us are perfect, we will have some strong and some weak areas. These are not bad, just insightful and should help us learn to value others that are different.

Learning to surround ourselves with a variety of personalities and styles will help everyone involved. Once we quit demanding uniformity and start appreciating differences, we will all grow more mature and Christ-like.

Most of us are simply too busy to stop and observe. This chapter's title includes the word, "Discovering," and that is what we must do. As we stop and observe, evaluate and take the time necessary to reflect, we will learn. As you read this chapter, think about the last conflict situation you walked through. Think about the people involved and how you and they acted and reacted.

The Thomas-Kilmann Instrument:

To improve our awareness and understanding of ourselves and others, we frequently recommend the use of a conflict style assessment known as TKI, the Thomas-Kilmann Instrument.

This organization has done extensive research and development of the assessment that compares two basic inputs of behavior in conflict situations:

assertiveness, the extent to which the individual attempts to satisfy his or her own concerns, and **cooperativeness**, the extent to which the individual attempts to satisfy the other person's concerns.[8]

Measuring and assessing traits and preferences of these two axis points allows TKI to plot a person's tendencies across five specific behaviors of how people respond and attempt to manage conflict.

The five styles are labeled:

COMPETING
COLLABORATING
COMPROMISING
AVOIDING
ACCOMMODATING

---

[8] www.TAKETHETKI.com

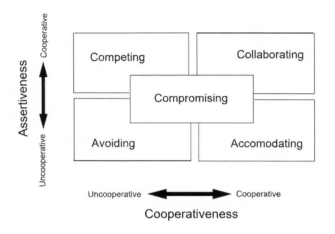

The graph has two axis's, assertiveness and cooperativeness. As a person's scores are plotted, they move up or down the continuum and tendencies begin to take shape. The data points show a relationship between assertiveness and cooperativeness. Following that plotting, a person can then begin to understand their own tendencies. It is likely that a person will have a primary leaning and a secondary leaning.

Beyond the labels and corresponding definitions, there are several keys to remember when reviewing ours and other's scores.

1) There is no one perfect style, regardless of how we feel about the labels and corresponding definitions. All styles are valid and can be effectively used, if we use it in the right place at the right time. If we only

use one style, our dominant style, you will limit your overall potential to navigate conflict.

2) Depending on the circumstances and what is at stake, all of us, at one time or another, have likely used all five styles.

3) A case could be made that Jesus used each of the styles in different situations. So, whatever your style, it is okay. Learn about it, embrace it, and then try flexing styles when prudent.

4) This tool and corresponding knowledge are to be used for increased understanding and respect for others, not to manipulate their behavior.

5) The purpose of this information is meant to move our ministries from dysfunctional conflict, to healthy functional conflict.

6) It is important that you don't try to label people based on your limited exposure to this material. Use the assessment and then discuss, teach and help the group move forward.

Now, to gain a basic understanding of different styles of dealing with conflict, we move to the definition behind the labels. The following material comes directly from the TKI assessment:

COMPETING - Competing is assertive and uncooperative, a power-oriented mode. When competing, an individual pursues his or her own concerns at the other person's expense, using whatever power seems appropriate to win his or her position. Competing might mean standing up for your rights, defending a position you believe is correct, or simply trying to win.

COLLABORATING - Collaborating is both assertive and cooperative. When collaborating, an individual attempts to work with the other person to find a solution that fully satisfies the concerns of both. It involves digging into an issue to identify the underlying concerns of the two individuals and to find an alternative that meets both sets of concerns.

Collaborating between two persons might take the form of exploring a disagreement to learn from each other's insights, resolving some condition that would otherwise have them competing for resources, or confronting and trying to find a creative solution to an interpersonal problem.

COMPROMISING - Compromising is intermediate in both assertiveness and cooperativeness. When compromising, the objective is to find an expedient, mutually acceptable solution that partially satisfies both parties.

Compromising falls on a middle ground between competing and accommodating, giving up more than competing but less than accommodating. Likewise, it addresses an issue more directly than avoiding but doesn't explore it in as much depth as collaborating. Compromising might mean splitting the difference, exchanging concessions, or seeking a quick middle-ground position.

AVOIDING - Avoiding is unassertive and uncooperative. When avoiding, an individual does not immediately pursue his or her own concerns or those of the other person. He or she does not address the conflict. Avoiding might take the form of diplomatically sidestepping an issue, postponing an issue until a better time, or simply withdrawing from a threatening situation.

ACCOMMODATING - Accommodating is unassertive and cooperative—the opposite of competing.

When accommodating, an individual neglects his or her own concerns to satisfy the concerns of the other person; there is an element of self-sacrifice in this mode. Accommodating might take the form of selfless generosity or charity, obeying another person's order when you would prefer not to, or yielding to another's point of view.[9]

Perhaps by now you have already had a few "ah ha" moments. You remember a person, a meeting, a conversation with your spouse or child where a point of conflict ensued. Now you have begun to recognize your tendencies. That's a good start! But as mentioned earlier, do not try to guess yours or others tendencies, rely on the assessment. Take the time and spend the money to do it right.

Just as a good Bible teacher instructs their students not to take Bible verses out of context and subsequently draw erroneous conclusions, we are asking you to practice the same principle here. Understand the whole person and

---

[9] www.TAKETHETKI.com

gain an understanding of the complete context. It will be worth your time and money to help your ministry move forward.

Here are the next steps to move your ministry from dysfunctional conflict to healthy, functional conflict:

1) Invest in a professional assessment for key leaders, ministry teams, and leadership groups. Hire a professional from the outside to guide your team through a process of learning. Ministry is too important to get bogged down or thwarted by a lack of knowledge and understanding. We are blessed today in so many ways because this type of knowledge is readily available if we take the time and make the effort.

2) Make room for all styles, God created them all, even the ones you don't like! Don't limit your ministry potential by just inviting those whom you always see eye to eye with.

3) Truly embrace and appreciate differences.
Remember the human behavior model presented in chapter 3? We need to use this information to move from ignorance/intolerance to tolerance of the various styles. We need to accepting other's conflict management style (even if it is different from our own) then hopefully, as we work with and through others to advance the Kingdom of God, we might actually start appreciating each other. When genuine appreciation takes root, then we can begin to really value people like Jesus did!

4) Once people sense and feel genuinely valued, you can begin to work together on a whole different plain. Will there still be the tension related to differing styles, probably. But it no longer has to evolve into a breakdown of communication or worse, keep the relationship and or ministry from moving forward.

By now you might be tempted to say "Wow, this is a lot to consider. This could mean a lot of work" and we would say yes, it is. But consider the alternative: continued dysfunctional conflict and all the problems, pain, time and baggage that accompanies it. Seems like a lot less painful to go ahead and take the time and money to get ahead of this problem that plagues most ministers and ministries. It is your choice.

Discussion/application questions:

1) Do the various styles make sense? Have you seen or felt them influence a conversation or conflict? Explain.
2) How can I or how can we (group) use this information?
3) How can I apply it to help myself grow and or how can we apply it and help our ministry flourish?
4) Are there any applications to my family/personal relationships using this information?

7. Board Relationships

Obey your leaders and submit to them, for they are keeping watch over your souls, as those who will have to give an account. Let them do this with joy and not with groaning, for that would be of no advantage to you. Hebrews 13:17

How's your church set up? Whether your congregation is a megachurch with a large staff or a single-staff ministry, you will have some sort of leadership team in place.

Perhaps an established group hired you. Maybe you set up the group as the founding leader. Regardless of how you arrived in your current situation, there you are, and you must learn how to navigate through this complex maze of personalities and conflict styles represented in this assembly of believers.

Each person sitting around the leadership table brings a set of strengths, weaknesses, giftings, and baggage.

Every one of us is a mixture of godliness and sinfulness. A church will typically not rise any higher or go any further than the leadership directing it.

Many church splits and disasters could be avoided if those in leadership simply learned how to work together as a team and appreciate one other instead of competing with each another.

In the Kingdom of God, there should be no room for self-centered, self-focused, self-loving leadership. The Kingdom we are building should be Christ's, not our own. Sadly, we all know this goal is yet to be achieved here on earth. Many churches have experienced the ravishes of power struggles, selfish leaders, and living under those that should loving lead, but spiritually abuse.

Learning how to successfully navigate through the board room is critical to any pastor that leads a church. Pastors typically love to preach, teach, and serve the church, but board meetings, administrative work, planning, and goal setting might drive them nuts.

Yet, without administrative leadership, the church will wander. God has established the concept of human authority over His Church. Whether we like it or not, in the Body of Christ we better learn how to not only get along with our fellow leaders, but actually love them and learn from them.

I (Glenn) have had the privilege over the years to serve on several Christian ministry and local church boards. I have served on three church boards, one Christian university board, one international missions agency board, one camp and retreat center board, and have reported to over a dozen boards through my contract CFO work. In total, at last count, I have attended just over 300 board meetings in my career! Sigh.

The boards I report to through my contract CFO work has afforded me the opportunity to observe and study boards, their composition, governance, interactions and how they function. I have witnessed well run meetings and boards that work together and are engaged, but unfortunately, that is not the norm. The vast majority of boards fall into one of three categories:

Scrutiny board – they exist to find fault, find out what's wrong, and who is at fault. They view themselves as "The Knights Templar" protecting the organization from all that is evil. They do little to help the organization move forward. They justify their role by saying "Someone has to hold people accountable and protect the mission."

Windy board – they tend to blow in, blow up and then blow out. They can be nosy and noisy, stir up a bunch of institutional dust, then before the dust settles, they have all gone back to where they came from (cities or their respective pews). They seldom produce any tangible value to the organization.

Passive board – aka rubber stampers, this board tends to put in their time, act interested, then rubber stamps staff and leadership's initiatives and call it good. They feel good about being on a board, but really don't contribute much.

One Christian non-profit board service that began with great joy, turned into one of the most ugly, destructive set of circumstances I have ever witnessed. Unfortunately, because of my position on that board, I was forced to navigate the group through the worst conflict I had ever witnessed.

There were a couple of board members who were grumbling about the CEO for various reasons. Then one board member took it upon themselves to do everything they could to bring the CEO down. Facts did not matter, only the agenda of firing the CEO mattered. What followed was a series of tactics that can only be construed as a witch hunt. Fear mongering, false accusations, and misconstrued events ruled the day. No amount of fact finding, or reason would change the course of this board member's agenda.

Fortunately, with strong and assertive leadership, the board employed Biblical principles, starting with Matthew 18. As the true facts came to light, this person's assault resulted in a Biblical board reprimand, a measure of personal shame and a public apology and restoration. Crisis averted, but at huge, unnecessary cost.

There is a heavy price to pay for this kind of destructive conflict. Even though it was technically a win, I don't think anyone in the room called it a win. While a sad series of events, questions need to be answered including: What could have made this a different process?
What could have changed the course of this conflict into something more constructive and certainly less destructive? Every event can turn into a lesson if we listen.

With all this dysfunction, then what does a high functioning board look like:

Functional and Engaged Board –

1) They have a heart for the vision and mission of the church. Not their vision and mission, the church's. I would add the following thought to this matter. If a board member cannot articulate the mission and vision with clarity, how can they effectively provide leadership to the church?

2) They learn, understand and stay current on the context of the organization. Through staff interaction and reports, observation, industry research, reading articles and books and other research material, they basically get up to speed on the organization and the context in which it lives. If you serve on a board of an inner-city church, then get up to speed on the context, what are the trends, what is going on in the community, what has been working across the country and what is not working? What are other denominations experiencing in this same context? The more you know, the more you can help.

3) They show up for meetings, prepared and engaged.

4) They spend time in regular prayer individually and together seeking God's plan for the future.

5) They are selfless in their service, not seeking anything in return, but seeking only to serve the organization.

6) They are cheerful givers! Oops, now we have gone to meddling. Yes, active, engaged board members should be leaders in giving. For example, a church client called one day asking for advice. They had a long-term church member who worked in a prominent position in the financial industry. They volunteered to be church treasurer. The board asked me if it was ok for him to be treasurer, even though he didn't contribute to the church! Seriously!!! I think you already know my answer.

7) They are a diverse group, including race, education or economic status, as well as diverse in personality and conflict management styles as discussed earlier. You want to see issues with 360-degree vision and the only way to accomplish that is to have a diverse board, truly representative of the congregation and or the community it is attempting to serve.

8) They get to really know each other's hearts. They get to know each other outside of the business of the board. They spend time together not solving the organization's problems, so when they come to work together, they have a more understanding view of their brothers and sisters.

9) They learn to really listen to each other, respect other's opinions and at times, agree to disagree. Recently I was serving on a board where the organization was facing persistent mission and financial challenges. Because the board was engaged and functioning fairly well, we were able to engage

in what I labeled, "Mature Christian adult conversations" about the tough issues. Without finding fault or criticizing, without blame shifting or scapegoating, we were able to examine some tough data and do a proper evaluation of the situation and then take appropriate action for the future. It was a God moment to be sure. Everyone was amazed at how redemptive the process was and walked away feeling like we made a difference! As discussed earlier, this was a far cry from a previous meeting where the board member tried to take down the CEO!

10) They are unified in their love for each other and a love for serving the organization. Nothing can usher in the presence of God faster than unity. For clarity, unity does not mean rubber stamping or passive involvement. In the successful board meeting mentioned above, unity among great differences prevailed and did indeed command a blessing!

So now that you know the top ten list of a functional board, go get it done! But wait, there may be a few steps involved.

As a practical means of developing a fully functional and engaged board we offer the following: (note the 1 – 10 matches up with the previous list of 1 – 10)

1) Choose/recruit your members carefully. Recruit for skills and abilities, but never at the expense of a heart for serving.

2) Choose/recruit lifelong learners. People that are open. People who are willing to put in the time to get up to speed and stay up to speed.

3) Choose/recruit people who you can count on to be there and invest the proper amount of time into the process.

4) Choose/recruit people of prayer. Someone once said, "prayer is the slender nerve that moves the mighty arm of God!"

5) Choose/recruit selfless servants of God, humble in spirit, tenacious in service.

6) Choose/recruit generous givers. Not to be determined by how much, but by their level of sacrifice, see the passage on the window's mite.

7) Choose/recruit a truly diverse board in race, gender, education, economics, and maybe even most important, diverse personality and conflict styles. Think globally, think 360-degree view.

8) Choose/recruit people who want to get along, want to know and be known, celebrate and be celebrated, and who seek to both understand and be understood (borrowed from Stephen Covey)

9) Choose/recruit members who know how to really listen and respect differences.

10) Choose/recruit members who understand the principle of Biblical unity and what it means to walk the talk.

Next Steps:

1) If you would like to test this list, and/or take the pulse of your leadership team, you have our permission to copy it and give it to board members and ask them to rank how <u>they</u> are doing in each category personally and how they think the <u>board</u> is doing in each category. Rank each item 1-10, with 10 being the best. Then tally the highest score for individuals and group, the lowest score for each and then the average. Might be a very interesting exercise/learning experience! What accounts for the differences between the highest scores and the lowest scores? Are you happy with the averages in each category? Talk about it!

2) Meet, review the data collected, and devise a customized plan as to how your group can maintain its strengths and work on its weaknesses.
That list might include items like:

- Do some expectations/accountability training
- Entertain some board resignations
- Recruit new board members
- Spend some regular time praying together
- Do some team building activities
- Do some communications, personality style or conflict style training

- Do a book study together
- Do some expectations/accountability training
- Eat together! It's in the Bible!

3) Formulate your own set of standards and expectations and be sure and include a set of accountability functions and corresponding consequences.

4) Then train, train again, and then retrain. It will take constant reinforcement.

The items on the top ten list, if taken seriously, will go a long way toward moving your organization's board toward functional conflict, the kind where "iron sharpens iron" for the good of the organization.

For those who are now looking at the list and saying in a sheepish winey voice "...But this would be hard, it will take too much time.... whaa, whaa...." we would answer "So much more a dysfunctional board fraught with conflict!" The question then becomes where do you want to spend your time? Once again, it is a choice you will make.

Finally, it should be noted here that you as a pastor or church leader do not have to know everything about effective boards or even be proficient at it. No one person can do it all. But understand with your new awareness of what needs to be done, you are responsible to deal with it. Since you know you can't do it all, recruit help, hire someone from outside the church, borrow someone from another church or get some help from a denominational office. Just do it.

Discussion/application questions:

1) Take the functional board 1-10 list and rank your board/leadership for each category listed, 1 -10, ten begin the highest.

2) Tabulate the highest rank, lowest rank and average for each category.

3) Examine and discuss the variances in opinions. (because there will be large perceived differences!) What is true, what is real or perceived, what are we seeing, what are we not seeing?

4) Look at next steps, which of the tips from this chapter need to be implemented?

5) Establish a time table and framework for board/leadership development, monitor it and evaluate as you go forward. After an appropriate time, do a reassessment to see if the scores have changed.

8. Staff Relationships

Tychicus will tell you all about my activities. He is a
beloved **brother** and **faithful** minister and fellow servant
in the Lord. Colossians 4:7

Regardless of the church size, none of us work alone.
We may be the only paid staff, but there are always those
who help carry the load of ministry. Perhaps a volunteer
secretary or maintenance person, maybe a part-time
treasurer or bookkeeper, regardless of who they are or if
the church pays them, they will be co-workers, and co-
laborers in Christ.

If we haven't learned anything else yet, if people are
involved, conflict will be as well. I (Jeff) served for over a
decade on a large church staff. We had multiple pastors,
support staff, and a large Christian school. The
opportunities for conflict were readily available and were a
regular part of church life.

Just imagine multiple pastors sharing one administrative staff member and all of them having pressing deadlines. On a weekly basis, it was my job to keep the peace, reassign priorities and help train all involved in basic Christianity! Hurt feelings abounded and each of us needed to learn how to think of others first.

Just because the people involved are Christians does not mean they are perfect or mature. Each of us struggles with insecurities, pride, wanting to be loved and to gain approval. When these are lacking in any fashion, conflict can and will take place.

Throw some budget restraints and facility space limitations into the mix, and even the godliest pastor or staff person will be challenged to remain calm and walk in agape love. We are creatures that battle with our flesh and just because we are serving on the same church staff or ministry team does mean we will not conflict with one another. In fact, the opposite is likely to take place.

In the church, there can be jockeying for acceptance of the senior leader(s). Myopia tends to take place among godly leaders that are driven and focused on accomplishing their ministry.

Most pastors, whether they serve youth, young marrieds, seniors, children or any number of ministry and worship roles, tend to think what they are doing is the most important ministry in the church. In some ways, that passion and focus is understandable and commendable. After all, why wouldn't everyone in the church love young people, old people, singles or children? Isn't music the main thing going on in heaven, and why wouldn't home groups be the most important ministry!

With everyone pushing their primary ministry as the best or most critical one, what could possibly go wrong relationally?

I (Glenn) have had and continue to have many conversations with senior pastor's asking what went wrong with this staff member or that congregation member.

For the sake of this chapter, we propose staff relationships operate on two planes: staff to staff, and staff to congregation. We also assume staff can be part time, full time, paid or volunteer.

In one of my (Glenn) roles as church administrator of a fast-growing church, we were very busy with amazing ministry initiatives at home and abroad. We were seeing people come to Christ, and others deepening their walk with our Lord. The cause and the busyness were nearly intoxicating. It became hard to slow down or stop climbing new mountains for the Kingdom.

One day I received a phone call from a church member who wanted to come by and ask some questions about an upcoming ministry outreach. I said "Sure, let's have lunch, I'll come your way."

When we first sat down, he very respectfully shared he was not only surprised I took his call, but then invited him to lunch. He went on to say he just assumed that I was too busy to take the time to meet with him personally, one on one. Ouch! I was taken back by his candor. I shared with him if I ever get too busy to meet with God's people, I have lost my way. Great answer. While it was true, I later had to ask myself and our staff what exactly are we communicating and conveying to our congregation?

We have observed over the years that ministry relationships can be enhanced in four areas of focus. There are certainly more than four, but these four tend to reduce conflict and enhance and encourage healthy relationships in ministry: (this includes staff to staff and staff to congregation members)

- Trust – Task and Relational
- Managing Expectations
- Monitoring Equity
- Valuing Others

Trust – Task and Relational

"Without trust, you have nothing. Trust is an increasingly rare commodity these days. People have become increasingly suspicious and skeptical. At one time, you could assume that others would trust you until you gave them a reason not to. But today with most people, you must prove your trustworthiness first."[10] John Maxwell, "Becoming a Person of Influence"

Sad but true. Honest people don't usually think about building and maintaining trust, but it is essential in ministry relationships. We go one step further in our analysis by breaking down trust into two categories: task trust and relational trust.

---

[10] John C Maxwell Becoming a Person of Influence, Thomas Nelson Inc, Nashville, 1997 Pg. 84

In ministry relationships (actually all relationships) people are often confused by what they perceive as mixed signals related to trust. One day you are a trusted co-worker, or church member, the next day an assignment you had lobbied for went to another staff member or church member. "What's going on? Once I was in the inner circle, now I am on the outside. Then, suddenly I get invited back into the inner circle, but only for a while. This is all very confusing!" Sound familiar?

Unknowingly, people have two trust buckets for every relationship, the task bucket and the relational bucket. Let me illustrate. In my first full time church administration position, I was viewed as a very task oriented, forward moving person and if you wanted something done, give it to me. BUT, stay out of my way, and certainly don't bother me with your feelings, the only thing that mattered was getting the job done. (Sounds a bit like a Mad Paddler doesn't it!?)

Well one day I was working with a local vendor who did not treat the church very well. I finally ended up writing him a rather curt email telling him what was what and this is how we were going to do business or else!

Unfortunately, the following week, the senior pastor called me in his office to review the email with me. The vendor was offended, and I came to find out the pastor was reaching out to him trying to share the gospel with him. He went on to instruct me as to how I was to properly and carefully conduct the business of the church.

It was one of the more painful ministry lessons I had to learn. I went on to do great things for the church and gain great "task trust" from the congregation and staff, but sadly, I continued to make "relational trust[11]" mistakes that kept many people at a distance.

Task trust is when people trust you in your work, your organizational skills, your specific technical skills, your ability to get things done. If there is a hard problem to solve or there is a crisis, they will knock on your door. This is a great bucket to fill!

Relational trust is when people trust you personally, your heart, your godliness, your empathy, your values, your biblical worldview. They would trust you with their kids! This is also a great bucket to have full.

Now, back to my first church administration position, high scores for Task trust, low scores for Relational trust. Because of my lack of understanding regarding the two buckets of trust, I was often confused and offended when I did not get assignments, I thought I was entitled to. Looking back, it is easy to figure out, they were not able to trust the relationship side of my ministry.

In one of my many church planting journeys' I worked with a pastor who was one of the most relational guys I had ever met. He was fun to be around, warm and friendly, had a great sense of humor, and was a very emphatic listener. He was by many measurements a great pastor.

Over the next two years, I lost trust in our relationship not because he lacked relational trust, he lacked task trust

---

[11] Task and Relational trust = Miller Management Systems, LLC, "Building Effective Relationships With Staff and Constituents" Page 15, June 2017

in our relationship. He would often say one thing and do another. (Really bad idea for anyone) He would often forget to follow-up on key church initiatives.

One time we were locked out of the school we were meeting in because he forgot to make the right contacts. Several times we had church without air-conditioning in the 95 plus degree heat because he forgot to have it turned on. And this "task" trust list of violations went on and on.

Eventually we left the church. He was very hurt and confused. At that time, I did not have enough understanding about the two sides of trust to explain it to him. To this day I love him, think he is a great guy, but I would never work with him again. (And yes, I understand he could have and should have delegated those tasks, but he would not) and so it goes.

What are the keys to managing task and relational trust in ministry to reduce conflict and enhance relationships?

1) Write down the top 3-4 things that are most important to you in each category, i.e. to trust a person in tasks I must see _____, and to trust a person relationally I must believe _____. Share your responses with your ministry team, compare with others, learn, discuss and decide how to build mutual task and relational trust set of values.

2) Look for signs of out of balance conditions and seek to balance them. Lower one and or cause the other to go higher. No relationship will ever be perfectly balanced, and it's okay to teeter a bit back and forth, but a grossly out of balance condition, will erode the

relationship over time and create mistrust for the totality of the relationship. You must become more proactive and purposeful if you find yourself out of balance.

3) Be observant. Talk with folks if you see or feel strain in the relationship, ask how they are doing. Also remember, based on personality, they may or may not tell you. You may have to ask more than once.

4) Be sure to consider each person's unique personality and conflict management style and how that plays into how they feel about their relationships.

5) Try to keep your side of the relationship in balance even if the other person isn't trying or hasn't read this book! That means sharing with supervisors, bosses, lay leaders, pastors, friends, etc. how you feel about the relationship and why.

6) Practice walking in the other person's shoes and asking yourself if you would like to be there. If not, adjust.

7) Remember that lopsided or out of balance trust will lead to relationship breakdowns over time.

8) Understand your own personal trust list.

9) Understand and respect other's personal trust lists.

10) Take time as an organization to define our corporate trust list.

11) Invest and try to help each other manage your respective lists. This means communicating effectively when those list items are violated. Early detection and communication can greatly reduce conflict and misunderstandings.

This won't be easy or altogether clear at times, but at least now you have a platform for exploration and discussion.

Managing Expectations

"Wow, I was really mad when I first heard you say that, but I was totally wrong, I thought you meant..." Sound familiar? It has been said the quickest way to conflict is to mismanage expectations.

I once had a car dealership regularly give me quotes on repairs, and every single repair came in under the quote. Eventually I found out it was their preferred method of managing expectations in customer service. Interesting, but somewhat deceptive/manipulative as a regular practice.

We measure conflict in relationships as the difference between **expectations and reality**. Those that are new to the church are disappointed when they learn that their highly impacting, humorous and engaging pastor in the pulpit is really an extreme introvert in person. Is that wrong or bad, no, just a difference between our expectations and reality.

How do we manage expectations more effectively?

1) Work on improving communications. Be clear, more proactive, anticipate what people will need and when they will need it. Remember:
   - Unclear expectations create frustration.
   - Unrealistic expectations set us up for failure.
   - Uncommunicated expectations are just not fair.

2) Anticipate gaps and attempt to bridge them before they happen. Aids for monitoring the gap for staff and congregation members include:
   - Have regular informal checkpoints on projects/tasks
   - LISTEN; hear their perspective and expectations
   - Communicate, communicate, communicate

What do you do when you see a gap exists? Based on real <u>or</u> perceived gaps, attempt to:

Alter their expectations OR alter reality (change your behavior)

To not manage expectations up front will most assuredly require you to manage the gap after the fact. Once again, it's a choice we all make as to when we will deal with the issues.

Monitoring Equity[12]
From a human nature standpoint, it appears most people strive for what they perceive as an "equitable"

---

[12] Monitoring Equity = Miller Management Systems, LLC, "Building Effective Relationships With Staff and Constituents" Page 34, June 2017

situation relating to their relationships in general. It begins at a very early age. As I observe my young grandchildren, I hear them say "That's not fair, it's my turn, I had it first!" They are very cognizant of attaining equity at a very early age.

While the context may change when studying work, home, and ministry life, the behavior appears to be consistent. The methods and behaviors people display in pursuit of equity varies greatly, but in the end, they are searching for real or perceived equity.

Example 1: Ministry staff:

I remember hiring a church bookkeeper that had been out of the work force for many years raising her children. She did not have a college degree. She seemed bright and energetic but would need a lot of training to bring her skills up to speed. So, we took a chance and hired her.

Over the next four years she learned quickly and did a very nice job. She also received higher than normal raises and was doing well. Then I recruited an experienced college graduate to be the administrative assistant to the senior pastor. She was highly qualified, many years of relevant service and came in and did a great job. Unfortunately, the wages paid to the new administrative person were slightly higher than the bookkeeper, which because of experience and a college degree, seemed to make pretty good sense.

The bookkeeper, who prior to the hire had been happy and productive, came to me with an ultimatum that went something like this: "If you don't give me a raise that puts me above her, I quit." I said without hesitation, "That is a shame, we are going to really miss you." She gave her notice and we moved on.

What happened to a happy productive staff member? Her perception of equity changed. Even though our move was justified, it produced a real or in this case perceived inequity.

Example 2: Congregation member

A wonderful volunteer for decades, Mrs. Wonderful decides to retire from her duties as the annual Valentines Banquet coordinator. For years she had made the job look easy. And each year it was a great success. (The names and circumstances have been changed to protect the innocent and the guilty!)

The following year her replacement, Mrs. Jane Q. Public took over. She rallied the troops, got out publicity, and worked extremely hard. A staff member's wife who just happens to live close to Mrs. Public, noticed the long hours and hard work, and thought they should publicly recognize her efforts. The banquet was a success, and at the end of the banquet, formal recognition was given. Sadly, Mrs. Wonderful walked away feeling under appreciated.

The problem is that we all have different measures of equity, so how can we possibly deal with these real and/or perceived expectations?

Let's look at some common equity or inequity pitfalls:

Staff members feel this real or perceived out-of-balance condition when:

- Hard work results in getting dumped on more often with no end in sight.
- Hard work goes unnoticed or unappreciated or unrewarded.
- Input not asked for or recognized even though contributions over the years have been significant.
- Perception that the staff member is giving far more to the church than the church is giving to the staff member (pay, recognition, kudos, esteem etc.)

Congregation members feel this real or perceived out-of-balance condition when:

- Hard work results in getting dumped on more often.
- Hard work goes unnoticed or unappreciated.
- Input not welcome, recognized or regarded.
- Real or perceived idea that their hard work is just not worth it.

Resulting staff or congregation member's behavior of real or perceived inequity includes:

- Hard workers get discouraged; they see no benefit to working hard.
- Slothful workers are content; they see no penalty for poor work.
- Important ministry ideas, concepts and possibilities can be lost forever.
- People leave in search of more "equitable" or satisfying relationships.

Key: When a real or perceived inequity is felt by an individual, i.e. their investment is perceived as greater than their return, it creates an out of balance condition and then certain negative behaviors occur.

By now you might be tempted to say "Well, they just need to get saved! They need Jesus. They need to grow up. They need to mature." While any or all of those may be true, it does not change the fact you must deal with it and meet them where they are. Jesus was pretty good about that.

Why do leaders make these kinds of equity mistakes and what are the consequences? Here are some common reasons leadership fall into this equity trap with staff and/or congregation members: Leaders measure other's work by their own personal standards, vs. what is realistic.

- Leader only sees partial work performance and draw flawed conclusions.

- Leader has a negative pre-disposition toward an individual based on history or someone they remind us of.

- Leader feels they themselves are not given enough credit for successes, and too much blame for failures.

- Leader feels underappreciated for the effort they themselves exert.

Corresponding results of a leader's real or perceived failures in equity assessment:

- Unfair or unequal treatment of certain staff and congregation members.

- Unequal treatment discourages staff and or congregation members.

- Prevents many staff and congregation members from reaching their God-given potential.

- They leave and seek more "equitable" situations elsewhere and the church losses some great people.

Next Steps forward include:

1. Be proactive and get out ahead of people's real and perceived areas of equity and inequity though setting proper expectations, (see earlier in the chapter). Realize they also change over time. Observe, ask, seek understanding for underlying behavior, it just might be a communications/expectations problem.

2. Your definition of equity is likely very different than other's definition. Extend grace and understanding for their lack of understanding your definition and try to understand and respect their definition. Communication is the key.

3. Be an equity equalizer not an exclusive "equity taker" **or** "equity giver." Balance is the key. Work as hard for other's equity as you do your own. If you have a propensity to only seek equity for others that is a trap that feels Godly but will eventually burn you out. Consider balancing that out as well. Seek equity for others and yourself. Randy Mayes, a good and very bright and Godly management consultant

friend of mine told me recently "Glenn, stop doing things "for" people and start doing things "with" people!"

4. Before real or perceived inequities develop into full blown conflict, recognize them early by checking and rechecking with staff and members. Asking good, open ended questions will often reveal equity gaps.

Valuing Others:

After we start to build trust and bring balance to our task and relational behaviors, we have done some good work on better managing expectations and we have begun to watch and monitor the "equity zone", we have then laid a solid foundation to really begin to value people in significant ways.

The Scriptures are filled with references regarding valuing people. These values are evident in both the Ten Commandments of Exodus 20:1-17 and the Great Commandment of Matthew 22:36-40! Jesus devotes a great deal of his teaching and preaching on how we should be treating others.

The bottom line: value people as God values them. *Easier said than done!*

Here's how we devalue people:

*   Impugning motives. Nothing pours gas on the fire of conflict like making assumptions about one's motives.

*   Withdrawing, fleeing conflict because we can't work it out, everyone loses.

- Degrading, belittling or berating comments to lower the other person or their position/opinion.

- Bringing up past behaviors

- Withholding information

- Inconsistent behavior (task or relational)

- Threatening or manipulative behavior

- Judging or criticizing

- Diminishing or trivializing

What would Jesus do? NONE of them!

So here are some practical ways we can value others by our general behavior toward them:

- Use good manners:
  - Say please and thank you.
  - Make eye contact.
  - Be on time to meetings and appointments.
  - Address people with respect.
  - Listen carefully, with few interruptions.
- Apply the golden rule.
- Invest in other people's emotional bank accounts.
- Seek first to understand, then to be understood.
- Respect their space and their property.
- Respect their walls - create an environment in which the other person can gradually take down their walls.

- Suspend Judgment.

- Value differences - when we value differences rather than make them the focus of our conflict, we create safety.

- Be trustworthy:
    - with others by treating them as valuable and vulnerable.

    - with yourself by acting in ways consistent with your own value and vulnerability.

- Speak their love language.

- Consider adopting a covenant of how a group will agree to treat each other.

- Attempt to view people as God views them.

Consider adopting a written Matthew 18 covenant with staff and or church members:

1. If I have a problem with another person, I will go to him/her privately.

2. If someone has a problem with me, I want him/her to come to me privately, and I will be open to hear what he/she has to say.

3. If someone has a problem with me and they come to you, send them to me and I'll do the same for you.

4. If someone hesitates to come to me, say, "I'll go with you. I'm sure they'll discuss this situation with you." I'll do the same for you.

5. Be careful how you interpret me. I'd rather do that.

6. I will be careful how I interpret you.

7. If it's confidential, I won't tell, unless someone is harming himself/herself or someone else.

8. I won't send or pay attention to unsigned letters or notes. Information should always travel with a person's name, so it can be cleared up, if necessary.

9. I will not manipulate; I will not be manipulated.

10. When in doubt, I will bring up my concern or question.

How can you appropriately show value to church staff? How can we regularly and consistently show our church staff we value them? *(Always keeping in mind individual love languages)*

- Retreats – Some for fun, some for work, and some combination of the two.

- One-on-one discussions/meeting times.

- Meals together.

- Visiting them in their ministry settings.

- Joint hospital calls.

- Travel – take different folks to conferences.

- Spending task and relational time together in an appropriate manner!

- Celebrate their victories – be happy for them.

- Written cards & notes.

- Affirm from the pulpit.

- Make birthdays and anniversaries special.

- Occasionally, cater to their specific likings.

- Consider different levels and types of appreciation
  - Administrative support staff
  - Pastoral, director or managerial staff
  - Both together at times

- Be creative, don't be rote, invest time and resources.

- Lighten up sometimes!

How can we appropriately show value to our congregation members?

- Regular, consistent and appropriate Recognition. Be creative! Not rote.

- Thank you
  - Cards
  - Bulletin announcements

- Pulpit announcements
- One-on-one
  - Meals together
  - Phone calls
  - Time together

- Showing empathy, really listen to their heart.

- Enlist their ideas and input.

- Have a public celebration as a group.

In light of the content of this chapter, please consider this quote from NLT Romans 12: 9-18:

Don't just pretend that you love others. Really love them. Hate what is wrong. Stand on the side of the good. Love each other with genuine affection and take delight in honoring each other. Never be lazy in your work, but serve the Lord enthusiastically. Be glad for all God is planning for you. Be patient in trouble, and always be prayerful. When God's children are in need, be the one to help them out. And get into the habit of inviting guests home for dinner or, if they need lodging, for the night. If people persecute you because you are a Christian, don't curse them; pray that God will bless them. When others are happy, be happy with them. If they are sad, share their sorrow. Live in harmony with each other. Don't try to act important, but enjoy the company of ordinary people. And don't think you know it all! Never pay back evil for evil to anyone. Do things in such a way that everyone can see you are honorable. Do your part to live in peace with everyone, as much as possible.

Discussion questions/application:

Note, this chapter's length and content will require multiple sessions to dissect, debrief, and come up with an action plan.

For each section:

1) Does this section have truth in it that we need to apply? If so, what?
2) What are the key concepts that will help us move forward?
3) How to we proactively apply this information to us, our teams and our ministry?

9. Committees, Politics, and Volunteers

Your people will offer themselves freely on the day of your power, in holy garments; from the womb of the morning, the dew of your youth will be yours. Psalm 110:3

Most churches have multiple committees and are supported by hosts of volunteers. In fact, without those that freely give and support the work, there would be little actually accomplished.

Along with the blessing of expanding the work accomplished, comes the potential for conflict in multiple directions. From feeling overworked, overlooked, or under appreciated by church leadership to infighting and territorial battles, volunteers bring a wonderful opportunity for growth along with some unique challenges!

Committees also come with benefits and liability. Many committees have a life of their own and often take on a personality, thus creating even more opportunities for conflict and competition. While some competition may be healthy, an over abundance can destroy a church.

106

Since pastors and staff will regularly deal with volunteers and committees, it is helpful for these leaders tolearn the underlying principles of how to work with them. Depending on the skills and aptitude of church leaders to work with these unpaid groups, volunteers and committees will either enhance the ministry or become relationships to be dreaded.

Another aspect to be aware of is politics. No, not Red or Blue, but something far worse. Power grabbing, manipulation, fear mongering and worse can all be experienced under the heading of church politics.

What do church politics look like?

- When members lose sight of what is best for the church or ministry and become more obsessed with winning at any cost, we have entered the political realm.
- When members insist everyone must do exactly what they want or else they will take their money and go home, we have entered politics.
- When members pout, back bite, spread rumors and strife against others in the church, we have begun to play politics. We, have also sinned.
- When members start a rebellion to assure a committee, leader or pastor does not get their way, we have become political.

The Apostle Paul said:

To have lawsuits at all with one another is already a defeat for you. Why not rather suffer wrong? Why not rather be defrauded? 1 Corinthians 6:7

When members will choose to win at any cost and refuse to be wrong, we are in a dangerous place, and so is the church.

The Details:

The church is dependent on believers who give freely of their time and talents. In an ideal world, volunteers recognize their service to be a stewardship of all God has given to them by way of talents, gifts and abilities. However, not all volunteers work out. Some are simply serving in the wrong capacity.

To paraphrase Jim Collins, they are in the wrong seat on the right bus. Others may not be qualified for their volunteer service.

A worst-case scenario would be a sex offender leading a children's ministry. There are others who serve out of the wrong motivation, such as a desire for control or succumbing to peer pressure from a nominating committee.

So, what does one do when a volunteer or committee member is not working out? A common adage says, "you can't fire someone who works for free." Not only is this untrue, it is unwise. It is true churches and leaders should recognize and appreciate volunteers are not compensated. But they should also realize volunteers are anything but "free." Every volunteer--whether a Sunday School teacher, elder, committee member or uncompensated staff member--comes at a cost. It is often helpful to consider some of the hidden costs of volunteers.

The Real Cost of Volunteers:

Recruitment and training:

Finding the right volunteer takes time. Developing and reviewing the task description and recruiting the right person require both time and effort, a cost that must be anticipated.

Once on-board, volunteers need additional training, support and supervision. Often, paid staff provide this supervision, which means a real cost to the church. Add to this this the cost of background checks and, in some cases, additional insurance coverage, and the cost of volunteer ministry can quickly add up.

Resources:

Volunteers need a place to serve, whether a classroom, office, desk, computer, or vehicle and basic supplies. Starting a new ministry, even with volunteers, is expensive. An auditorium or gymnasium can easily cost $50/hour to heat or cool. The cost of "volunteer ministry" should include the resources it takes to support the ministry.

Regular Communication:

Most volunteers help once or twice a week. Effective and regular communication is essential. Whether this means weekly emails or phone calls, or face-to-face meetings, this is time paid staff will need to spend when using volunteers.

Recognition:

A volunteer task description will not likely include recognition, but studies show that recognition is essential if an organization wants to maintain high volunteer retention rates. Recognition activities like lunches, gift-cards or awards are a necessary cost for most successful volunteer programs.

Understanding volunteers are uncompensated, but not free, means volunteers who do not adequately fulfill their task are a poor stewardship, and need to be rehabilitated or removed.

Firing a volunteer is not easy, therefore a process to restore and remove volunteers will minimize the potential for conflict following the removal of a volunteer.

Here are six steps that can help retain your volunteers.

1. **Re-Enforcement.** You may have a volunteer who doesn't understand the guidelines that are established and must be followed. This is a common problem for churches that utilize youth and collegiate volunteers, some of whom automatically 'test' the rules as part of their self-expression. Reinforcement of the expectations may end the problem.

2. **Re-Train.** Send the volunteer back for a second education. Some people take longer than others to learn new techniques. Some may require a different training approach, such as one-on-one mentoring rather than classroom or video lectures. If the problem is lack of knowledge rather than lack of motivation, then work to provide the knowledge.

3. **Re-Assign.** Transfer the volunteer to a new position. For example, a VBS volunteer not performing during the Bible story time may excel at helping with refreshments. It is possible to misread the skills or inclination of a person. It also might be they are not getting along with the staff or other volunteers with whom they are working. Try them in a new setting: and see what happens.

4. **Re-Vitalize.** If a long-time volunteer has started to malfunction, they may just need a rest. This is particularly true with volunteers who have intense jobs, such as youth leaders or standing committee leaders. The volunteer may not realize or admit they need a break, but the wise leader

seeks to ensure the volunteer maintains his or her vitality.

5. **Refer.** Maybe they just need a whole new outlook of life. Swap your volunteers among ministries for a few months and let them learn a few new skills.

6. **Retire.** Some volunteers may reach a diminished capacity in which they can no longer do the work they once did and may even be a danger to themselves and to others. Give them the honor they deserve and ensure they don't end their volunteer careers in a way they will regret. Assist them in departing with dignity before the situation becomes a tragic crisis.

Sometimes, even after one or more of the steps above have been taken, the volunteer is unable or unwilling to perform their assigned task. Occasionally an offence such as theft, sexual harassment, physical abuse or actions that contradict the values or mission of the ministry will require immediate removal. The church should have a clear list of offenses that result in immediate termination of a volunteer.

At times, the issues are not as clear, such as a volunteer who frequently shows up late, lacks motivation or only begrudgingly follows instructions. In these cases, leaders need to consider the following five questions before terminating a volunteer:

- Is the volunteer creating significant added work for the paid staff?
- Is the volunteer causing the church or ministry to have a bad reputation?
- What are the benefits and liabilities of keeping the volunteer?

- Is there another person who could step in if the volunteer is removed?
- What has been done to change the behavior or attitude of the volunteer?

As a 24-year-old youth minister, I (Rodney) provided oversight to three program directors. The largest program was our Royal Ambassadors (boys 6-18), followed by the Girls in Action (girls 6-18) and Mission Friends (children) ministries.

Two of the directors were maturing believers with a heart for discipleship. Both came prepared and followed the curriculum, which provided a balance of Bible study, prayer, activities and skill development.

The other leader, Darlene, liked to supplement the curriculum with her own material—often as a substitute for the Bible study. She was often late, and frequently needed a ride to get to church.

One Wednesday evening, Darlene and girls were nowhere to be found. While some parents waited anxiously in their cars, others stood impatiently on the church steps. After 30 minutes, Darlene and the girls arrived, having returned from a fast food restaurant down the road.

Darlene unapologetically explained to parents the girls needed a break from the usual routine, so a trip to Hardee's for ice cream was in order. After the children left, I "fired" Darlene. The following Wednesday, Darlene was back.

In hindsight, my approach failed at many levels. Let's put this to the five-question test:

- *Is the volunteer creating significant added work for the paid staff?* No, Darlene was an ongoing frustration, but she was not causing a "significant" workload to me or any of the other staff.

- *Is the volunteer causing the church or ministry to have a bad reputation?* Darlene's activities were not helping to build up our reputation as a Gospel focused church, however, the girls in her group loved her, and the parents put up with her.

- *What are the benefits and liabilities or keeping the volunteer?* At the time, the benefits of her staying didn't come to mind. If I would have taken time to reflect and pray, I would have come to a more balanced understanding of Darlene's potential.

- *Is there another person who could step in if the volunteer is removed?* One liability I overlooked was "who would replace her." It was this factor that resulted in the senior pastor calling Darlene and asking her to continue as director.

- *What has been done to change the behavior or attitude of the volunteer?* Here is where I really failed. Unlike Jethro, who went to Moses with a concern--and a solution, I only raised concerns with Darlene. I failed to listen as much as I failed to train.

A final thought on volunteers: "So whatever you wish that others would do to you, do also to them, for this is the Law and the Prophets." (Matthew 7:12).

The first part of this verse is often referred to as "The Golden Rule." But it is in the second part of this verse we are reminded the law and words of the prophets continually stressed the need for impartially, love and compassion.

How we handle uncompensated ministry leaders clearly impacts church unity and, if handled well, will reduce the opportunity for conflict.

Discussion/application questions:

1) Have you ever had any conflict with a volunteer? How was it resolved? What could have been handled differently?
2) How would you define church politics? Does the church you serve at have any? Do they need to be evaluated or changed?
3) Does the church you serve have any policies regarding volunteers and/or board members regarding conflict? Should it?
4) Does the church you serve have any policies regarding retirement or volunteer removal? Should it? How about board members?

10. The Five "D's" of Managing Conflict

When you find yourself, your staff, congregation members, board members or any combination of the above, in the middle of conflict. What do you do?

The following process[13], while lengthy and at times complex, when properly adapted to each unique situation, can help everyone navigate the process.

We have all probably used and or experienced common (ineffective) methods of dealing with Conflict

- Ignoring Approach
- Yelling/Outbursts/Displays of Anger Approach
- Pressures Tactics/Force/Bigger Hammer Approach
- Logical Case Building/Debate Approach
- Attorneys and Court System/Legal Approach

---

[13] The Five "D"s = Miller Management Systems, LLC, "Results Oriented Conflict Management" Page, page 12, October 2007

None of these tend to end well for anyone, so maybe there is a better approach.

The Five "D's" of Resolving Conflict

One guiding principle is to try to resolve conflict at the lowest level possible! In my (Glenn) organization, Miller Management, we talk with staff and our clients about dealing with issues when they are a 1-2% problem, not an 80-90% problem." Deal with things early and often!

DISCERN	<ul><li>Is it really conflict?</li><li>Are the 3 ingredients present?</li><li>Is it interpersonal, within a team, or between teams?</li><li>Is it a power, rights, or position bargaining contest?</li><li>What is my natural style?</li><li>What mode matches the moment?</li><li>Do I need to intervene?</li></ul>
DEFUSE	<ul><li>Calmly acknowledge the conflict as it happens</li><li>Treat feelings as facts</li><li>Don't walk away</li><li>Don't power play</li></ul>

DETERMINE APPROACH	• Competing • Accommodating • Avoiding • Compromising • Collaborating
DISCUSS	• Contract for time • Preparing for the discussion • Laying ground rules • Facilitating the discussion
DOCUMENT	• Behavior contracts • Performance evaluations

I. Discern

Step 1: Stop and take the time to properly discern the situation. Is it a conflict or is it a difference?

"Differences" include:

- A difference of <u>opinion</u> or point of view
- A difference in <u>style</u> or preference (personality, problem solving, conflict handling style)
- A different <u>method</u> or process (different from yours!)
- A different interpretation (than <u>yours</u>!)

- A <u>communication</u> breakdown creates differences that are not present, just perceived

If it is a difference, handle the difference with maturity and the fruits of the Spirit!
- Patience
- Peace
- Love
- Understanding

At the right time and place, talk it through, ask questions, try to gain perspective and understanding. People will generally respond very well to open ended, thoughtful questions designed to gain understanding and perspective. This method can usually go a long way toward resolving "differences."

Actual Conflict:
- An <u>offense</u> has been taken
- A person feels <u>threatened</u>; physically, emotionally, spiritually
- A person feels emotionally <u>injured</u> or hurt
- Strong feelings of <u>anger</u> and/or frustration are present for a prolonged period
- <u>Unforgiveness</u> is present
- A person perceives they have been treated <u>unjustly</u>

Understand Conflict Drivers:

1. <u>Facts or Data</u> – when two parties simply have different information

2. <u>Processes or Methods</u> – when there is a difference of opinion over how things should be done

3. Goals or Purpose – when two parties cannot agree on a common goal

4. Values – when the parties disagree about basic meanings

Also Consider is this a task or relational oriented conflict?

Defining the conflict driver can assist you in developing the best response or approach to the conflict.

If it is truly a conflict, move to step 2.

Step 2: Are the 3 key ingredients necessary for dysfunctional conflict present?

Interdependency

The first ingredient generally needed to cause real conflict is when co-workers or co-laborers must *depend* on each other to accomplish their work or to be successful in their ministry, whether paid or volunteer.

The higher the dependency, the more impacting the conflict can become. Conversely, the less impact a co-worker's or co-laborer's behavior or work has on an individual, the less chance for conflict.

Blame

Coworkers/co-laborer who routinely shift blame or refuse to accept responsibility for workload, issues of conflict or problems in the workplace, typically find themselves in more frequent conflict situations.

Anger

Anger is generally propagated by lingering feelings of injustice, unequal treatment, favoritism, unresolved offenses, feelings of abandonment or simply just not doing what they want you to do! They are emotionally upset, possibly sending destructive verbal and non-verbal signals to each other.

By understanding which of the factors are contributing to the conflict, you can then better prescribe solutions for yourself and for others.

If one or more of the above ingredients are present, proceed to step three; if not, you may just have differences, see step one.

Step 3: Discern who is involved

You want to avoid involving folks who are not really involved. Avoid the temptation to gossip, huddle or otherwise validate your conflict with others who are not involved.

Don't allow your personal need for validation or being consoled to trump doing what is right Biblically and what is best for the conflict!

Interpersonal:

Is the conflict between <u>two</u> individuals?

Within a Team:

Are there <u>multiple individuals</u> in conflict? If so, are they factions or groups within the team or department? Be certain you understand the dynamics of the conflict by who is and is not involved.

Between Teams:

Is the nature of the conflict along <u>departmental</u> or ministry team lines? Once again, be certain you understand the dynamics of the conflict by who is and is not involved. Also understand groups behave differently from individuals! (Unruly groups are often referred to as mobs!)

Once you have properly diagnosed who is involved, move to step 4.

Step 4: Discern what type of contest this really is.

Power Struggle

Those in conflict use their resources (physical strength, threats, influence, corporate authority, allies, money etc.) to coerce or <u>intimidate</u> opponents.

Rights Competition

Those in conflict enlist a source of <u>authority</u> (parents, manager, judge, policy, etc.) to determine their rights are more legitimate than their opponents' rights and therefore should prevail.

Position Bargaining

Those in conflict, with or without the involvement of a neutral third party, participate in non-adversarial dialogue with the intent to reconcile - and preserve - contradictory

<u>positions</u>. This contest is normally won by those with superior debating skills.

II. Defuse

Once properly discerned, you can then move toward defusing the conflict.

Pre-empt conflict when possible

- What are the potential conflicts (People? Topics? Events?)
- Provide up-front communication or clarification to defuse the matter before it becomes a conflict.

When conflict happens anyway . . .

1) <u>Calmly</u> acknowledge dysfunctional conflict *as it happens*!

  - Simply calling attention to it frequently prevents it from worsening.

2) Treat feelings as <u>facts</u>

  - Frame emotional acts and words as objective, factual information.
  - It's easier to deal with "facts" than "feelings" and it honors human emotions.

3) Don't <u>walk</u> away

  - Don't ignore the conflict or hope it will disappear if you do!

4) Don't <u>power</u> play

- Don't abuse your authority as a manager to render on-the-spot judgments
- Reject the traditional management mentality of "don't bring your personal feelings to work!" People are people...they are emotional beings.

5) Use <u>humor</u>

- But use it wisely and appropriately!
- Be careful not to insult or downplay someone's emotions by your humor.

6) Respond with <u>serenity</u>

- Develop emotional self-control
- Don't give yourself permission to blow up, or people around you will bottle conflict to avoid your blow up, ultimately making the conflict worse!
- Use it as a challenge to be overcome, that you will demonstrate self-control during high conflict situations

7) <u>LISTEN!!</u>

- Listening communicates respect, kindness, and care

III. Determine Approach

1. Understand your unique mode of dealing with conflict.

The Thomas-Kilman Conflict Mode Instrument discussed in chapter six is an excellent tool to gain further understanding into our preferred style of handling as well as understanding other's styles of handling conflict.

Remember the five basic personal styles of handling conflict:

- *Competing*
- *Accommodating*
- *Avoiding*
- *Compromising*
- *Collaborating*

Q: Which style did Jesus use?

A: All of them!

<u>Key</u>: Your success in handling conflict will not be determined by which style you are proficient at or most comfortable with; it will be determined by how effectively you utilize the various styles at the right place at the right time.

2. Determine the level of involvement needed to effectively resolve the conflict.

It is important to understand the level of involvement that will most effectively deal with the issues at hand. Think carefully about your options before deciding how to intervene, if at all.

Ignore – sometimes the most effective method is to <u>ignore</u> it. Let the small issues work themselves out if possible. Use only when effective!

Self-Mediation

<u>One</u> of the parties involved in the conflict initiates steps to resolve the issues. If properly trained, and to the extent people involved see the value of this process, it can be a very successful model. If conditions are appropriate, do not be afraid to coach folks through this process.

Manager Mediation

The <u>manager</u> of the parties involved in the conflict initiates and facilitates steps to resolve the conflict.

This process is utilized when the parties are unable or unwilling to resolve the conflict through self-mediation, or the timeframe necessary for resolution is very short by necessitating circumstances.

Team Mediation

A highly <u>skilled</u> neutral mediator - or a highly skilled member of one of the teams in conflict - initiates and guides a structured process to seek resolution between the teams and or departments. This should be done by those trained and skilled in the process.

IV. Discuss

If it is diagnosed that a meeting between individuals or teams is necessary, then use the following tools to be as effective as possible.

1) <u>Invite</u> each individual to the conflict mediation discussion

- Ask each participant to attend a meeting to be facilitated by you
- Meet face to face
- Confirm in writing if necessary

2) Strategically choose the <u>site</u> for meeting

- Avoid "turf"
- Ensure privacy
- Avoid embarrassment

3) Allow for <u>open</u>-ended time commitment

- The discussion should continue long enough to find a solution or clear next steps.
- Don't artificially cut off the talk because the clock strikes "x."
- Be sensitive to hour of day and day of week re: energy levels
- Also know when to stop, look for good progress/closure points

4) Hold preliminary <u>meetings</u> with everyone

- Dispassionately describe what you know about the situation
- Listen
- Ask open ended questions
- Clarify
- Suspend judgment
- Tell them a joint meeting is forthcoming

5) Define the problem

- After hearing from all parties, define the problem specifically.
- What is the "real" problem or issue?
- Then define the problem to be resolved, but not HOW it will be resolved.

6) Describe success

To help establish a clear vision for the desired result, and document in writing what success looks like:

- What specifically have we identified as the key issue(s)?
- What is each person's part in the conflict?
- What specifically is each person going to commit to doing to help resolve the conflict and or move the relationship forward? It needs to be
  - ✓ behaviorally specific,
  - ✓ mutually acceptable
  - ✓ and defines each person's future accountabilities.

7) Define the ministry implications

- If this problem is not resolved, the ministry will be affected in the following ways...
- No "threats" about their personal futures, but if there are future implications, they must be presented in a factual manner

8) Manage the meeting

Pray... Not as a ritual, or out of routine, but genuinely spend time asking God for wisdom.

Insist on ... Direct dialogue between/among the parties in conflict.

Set parameters... Discussion "by the rules," no walking away, no one-sided solutions, no power plays, no extraneous topics.

Suggested Rules:

- Be honest, and expect honesty from the other person
- Share emotions using "I" statements rather than "You" statements
- Agree that disagreeing is OK
- Avoid resolutions that are too quick; people need time to process their thoughts and emotions, to pray about it, and to process possible solutions
- Avoid name calling
- Avoid threatening behavior
- Avoid reacting to emotionally-charged comments made by the other person
- Avoid putting the other person's position or their character down. *You can't expect someone to see eye to eye with you when you're looking down on them!*

Deal with one issue at a time ... Current conflict may be a result of previous conflict not dealt with.

Tips for the Discussion:

- Reflect on how you want to be viewed when the conflict is over!
- If you become frustrated, try taking the opposing view/perspective and defending it.

What the <u>Leader</u> Says & Does:

- Open the meeting by re-stating the problem as you have defined it
- Review the implications of letting the situation persist
- Explain your role as mediator - a conversation facilitator
- Reiterate the problem must be resolved by them, not by you
- Ask for someone to volunteer to begin the conversation. Then be quiet!

What to <u>Listen/Watch</u> for:

- Departures from the topic - no "dredging up" history or unrelated issues

- Changes in behavior that could mean further conflict (e.g. a talkative person becomes quiet, or a generally tactful person becomes tactless, etc.)

- Conciliatory gestures, including apologies, admissions of mistakes, and positive comments about the other person(s)
- Breakthrough moments - when there is a mutual exchange of conciliatory gestures, signaling an attitudinal shift from "me against you" to "us against the problem."

When to Seek <u>Resolution</u>:

- When a spirit of conciliation has been attained, intervene to suggest a "resolution" might now be possible

- Describe what success looks like: balanced, mutually agreeable, behaviorally specific, and defines future accountabilities

- Act as scribe, tell them they will each get a clean copy, and hold a brief "signing ceremony" to reinforce the spirit of cooperation (if necessary)

Conflict *resolution* isn't always the goal! Conflict *management* can produce a more effective ministry!

Bonus Section - Communication Pointers[14]

When sending communications, aka talking with someone, it is important to remember some specific pointers to help facilitate a healthy and productive conversation:

1) **Begin positively**. Try to begin most conversations with something positive. Be observant, look for the good in a situation or some portion of the project or process that you can give recognition for. To be effective, it must be genuine and specific.

2) **Communicate cause and effect** – State specifically what you have observed and the effect it is having. Relate your observations to actions, not personality, intelligence or

---

[14] Communications tips - Miller Management Systems, LLC, "Effective Personal, Team and Organizational Communications" Page 15 April 2007

style; simply state the facts. Then, communicate and illustrate the corresponding result.

C – Circumstance or Situation

A – Action

R – Result

E – Evaluation

3) **Create two-way dialog** – make certain the person you are communicating with feels comfortable in responding. Ask open-ended questions, encourage dialog, and ask for their observations or opinions.

4) **Generate ideas and solutions together** – point the conversation to generating solutions for improving the future. Examine multiple options. See if there is opportunity to agree on trying out a solution(s).

When receiving – remember to...

1) **Focus on the message, not the messenger** – we may not always like or appreciate the person or the delivery style, but every piece of communication has something important embedded in it. It is our job to dig out the communication and throw the wrapper away.

2) **Listen calmly and attentively** – show respect for the individual and what they are attempting to communicate. Often this will have a calming effect on the process for both sender and receiver. Don't prepare your response while acting as if you're listening! Wait three seconds before responding to anything the other person has said.

3) **Clarify feedback without defending or over-explaining** - restate what you have heard as clearly as possible by acknowledging their concerns in a recap format. Ask if you have understood what they were attempting to communicate. Ask for further concerns or details. This process extends value to the person and lets them know with certainty you understand what they are communicating.

4) **Ask for suggestions** – after acknowledging the other person's concerns, ask for suggestions or ideas as to how to improve the situation. Dialog about potential solutions and agree to what the next step in the process will be.

When addressing difficult issues remember to:

- **Choose a good time** – sometimes our timing can really enhance the conflict resolution process. Poor timing can certainly hurt the process. It could be that you will need to exercise patience and wait for the best time to address an issue.

- **Make an appointment** – ask for time to discuss an issue, give parameters of the discussion and approximately how much time you will need. Be courteous and respectful.

- **Go into the conversation with openness** – yes you have an issue or an agenda but be open and receptive to the responses of the person you're talking with. You might learn something new that changes the situation.

- **Be a good listener** – listen at least as much as you speak. Dialog, don't have a one-sided conversation.

- **Avoid blaming** – look for solutions, not blame. Use "I" not "You", don't put the other person on the defensive.

- **Validate** – at the appropriate times, summarize keys points you have heard and ask for additional insights.

- **At the end of the conversation, agree on the next step in the process** - don't leave a disagreement on the table, find a next step to agree on, even if it is only when you will meet again to discuss the topic further.

When working with <u>difficult people</u> remember to...

1) **Discern their initial position** – consider the other person's probable personality profile (DiSC), how they might be viewing and approaching the situation.

2) **Be consistent** – consistency builds trust and respect. Difficult people do not like surprises, they view them as additional reasons for mistrust.

3) **Refer mainly to your behavior** - pointing fingers and blame shifting encourages negative responses.

4) **Move forward** – to achieve greater influence and success, you must forget the past and move forward looking for better behavior.

5) **Be patient** – don't look for instant recognition or a word of thanks. Bad behavior is a pattern that takes a long time to change. Even if people see the change and like it, egos might prevent thanking those responsible.

6) **Reinforce good behavior** – when you see progress, be diligent to reinforce the good behavior, in public or in private, whichever is most appropriate.

V. Document

If the situation requires documentation based on the seriousness of the conflict, the lingering nature, or the significance if unresolved, then documentation may be necessary.

A Behavior Contract

Here's what I (the manager/leader/pastor) observed:

_____

_____

Here's when and where I observed it:

_____

_____

This is how it created problems for those involved:

_____

_____

Here's what Person "A" thought was fair:

_____

_____

Here's what Person "B" thought was fair:

_____

_____

Here is what we agreed would happen in the future: *(include specific instructions for who is to do what, by when, for how long, with whose support and cooperation, in what ways, etc.)*

_____

_____

If this contract is honored, the positive consequences will be:

_____

_____

If this contract is broken, the negative consequences will be:

_____

_____

Signed by leader _____

Signed by parties_____

Important Ministry Moment!

It doesn't matter whether you're right or wrong. The most impact comes from _how you handle_ a situation of conflict. People won't necessarily remember the outcome of a conflict years down the road, but they will remember *how you made them feel* and whether their stock *rose or fell with others*.

It is important to remember sometimes we attempt to resolve spiritual issues with logic and good practice. While logic and good practice can produce good results, there will be times spiritual issues cannot be dealt with by logic alone.

When the temptation arises to deal with a spiritual conflict with conventional weapons, stop and ask yourself:

Do you want the fruit of the law to prevail or do you want the fruit of the Spirit to prevail?

Then decide what spiritual fruits need to be exhibited to help resolve the issues at hand.

One final thought: If the spiritual issue cannot be resolved, there are cases for separation, folks moving on and changing venues, etc.

Concept provided with permission by: Timothy M. Gustafson, Gustafson Counseling & Consulting

Discussion/application questions:

1) What are the key learning points in this chapter?
2) Should we adopt the Five "Ds"?
3) If so, why or why not?
4) If yes, how do we train our staff, leaders, members?
5) How do we apply the concepts?
6) How can we use the communications bonus section?

Section III: The Spiritual Side of Managing Conflict

11. Pretenders, Dividers, and Obnoxious People

And no wonder, for even Satan disguises himself as an angel of light. 2 Corinthians 11:14

Not everyone who proclaims the name of Christ is a Christian. Not everyone who serves as a leader is qualified to lead. The Church is a mixture of both good and bad seed. There are those with wicked agendas and those that simply are obnoxious. Some sneak into the gatherings to sow strife and discord and others just rub most people the wrong way. How we deal with these people will impact the ministry.

Let's look at some categories of church members that may need some attention: pretenders, dividers, and those who have unfulfilled callings.

Pretenders:

Every church has those who cause trouble, but how do we deal with them in a God honoring fashion? How do we effectively deal with destructive people with personal agendas, ego maniacs, self-focused people, and those who seek to dominate leaders and fellow members?

When asked, "Why are there antagonists in the church?" my (Rodney) answer is simply, "Because they are in the world."

Effective organizations have in place clear processes to deal with those who seek to harm the church. Some are pretenders, such as Simon (Acts 8:9-24). These are people who profess to be Christians but are pretenders.

John Piper says of Simon (and as a warning to the Church today) "there is a 'faith,' there is a 'believing,' that does not save, even though it rises in the presence of true preaching and true miracles."[15] Such was the case of Simon.

At face value, he looked good—he professed belief, he was baptized, and he hung around the church. Below the surface, he was an unregenerate pretender who had no part in the Body of Christ.

Imagine the conflict that would have arisen if the church leaders had not addressed this hypocrisy. Simon attempted to use his wealth to influence the church. Sadly, pretenders exist in the church today. In fact, unregenerate church members may be the number one contributing factor when it comes to church conflict.

I (Rodney) am going out of a limb here, but the matter of pretenders is too important to leave hanging. When

---

[15] John Piper, *Simon's Prevision of the Signs and Wonders*, sermon preached May 12, 1991.
https://www.desiringgod.org/messages/simons-perversion-of-signs-and-wonders

considering whether unregenerate members are hindering the work of your church, prayerfully reflect on God's word:

- By this all people will know that you are my disciples, if you have love for one another. John 13:35
- Salvation is found in no one else, for there is no other name under heaven given to mankind by which we must be saved. Acts 4:12

- For I am not ashamed of the gospel, because it is the power of God that brings salvation to everyone who believes: first to the Jew, then to the Gentile. Romans 1:16

- For it is by grace you have been saved, through faith—and this is not from yourselves, it is the gift of God—not by works, so that no one can boast. Ephesians 2:8-9

- For the message of the cross is foolishness to those who are perishing, but to us who are being saved it is the power of God. 1 Corinthians 1:18

- Now, brothers and sisters, I want to remind you of the gospel I preached to you, which you received and on which you have taken your stand. By this gospel you are saved, if you hold firmly to the word I preached to you. Otherwise, you have believed in vain. 1 Corinthians 15:1-2

- Then he called the crowd to him along with his disciples and said: "Whoever wants to be my disciple must deny themselves and take up their cross and follow me." Mark 8:34

- Truly he is my rock and my salvation; he is my fortress, I will never be shaken. Psalm 62:2

- Or do you not know that wrongdoers will not inherit the Kingdom of God? Do not be deceived: Neither the sexually immoral nor idolaters nor adulterers nor men who have sex with men nor thieves nor the greedy nor drunkards nor slanderers nor swindlers will inherit the Kingdom of God.
  1 Corinthians 6:9-10

Do not overlook the power of a conversation. In my role as a Director of Missions, I (Rodney) was called upon by a church in rapid decline to meet with their pastor. During our initial meeting I asked him to share his story. The conversation went something like this.

Pastor: "Share my story? What do you mean?"

Rodney: "Your testimony, how you came to Christ and your call to ministry."

Pastor: "I've always been a Christian. My father and grandfather were pastors!"

Rodney: "But when did you experience God's saving grace and experience the new birth?"

Pastor: "I already told you, I've always been a Christian."

A few years ago, I started a replant church. One of the families from the original church was part of the core group. When the husband called to tell me he and his wife were divorcing, I asked if they would meet with me. In that meeting, I asked each one to share their testimony.

The wife shared of her upbringing as a preacher's kid and how, like everyone else in the church, she became a Christian at ten years old. This prompted some additional questions.

Apparently, her father understood the age of accountability to be ten years old, so he had every child that turned ten "pray the sinner's prayer." This was followed up by baptism the next Sunday. I am pleased to say the couple managed to stay together, and several months later the wife truly experienced the new birth. Today this couple has a vibrant ministry in evangelism and are key leaders in the church.

Both examples illustrate how unregenerate people can end up on the membership rolls.

If a church is unwilling to identify and deal with pretenders, they will find likely find themselves at odds with Acts 8:20, 1 Corinthians 5:11 or 2 Corinthians 6:14-15.

Dividers:

The next group to address is those who are dividers. Often, when unity is elusive, the issue is antagonists who relish in dividing the Church. Much of the following can be found in our book *Pastoral Helmsmanship*, and is based on "Antagonists in the Church" by Kenneth Haulk, who defines these dividers as follows:

Antagonists are individuals who on the basis of non-substantive evidence, go out of their way to make insatiable demands, unusually attacking the person or performance of others. These attacks are selfish in nature, tearing down rather than building up, and are frequently directed against those in a leadership capacity.

Let's start with a practical understanding of why we must identify and deal with antagonists in the church. **Unchecked, antagonists will make leading the church an impossible task**. The problem with antagonists in the church is they leave in their wake broken lives, broken dreams and discouraged, apathetic people. If this sounds like your church or group, then it is likely antagonists are present.

More important than the practical understanding is the biblical understanding, which instructs the believer to identify, confront and then avoid those who create conflict.

Identify

- Romans 16:17 - I appeal to you, brethren, take note of those who create dissentions and difficulties, in opposition to the doctrine which you have been taught.

- 1 Corinthians 1:10-12 - I appeal to you, brothers and sisters, in the name of our Lord Jesus Christ, that all of you agree with one another in what you say and that there be no divisions among you, but that you be perfectly united in mind and thought. My brothers and sisters, some from Chloe's household have informed me that there are quarrels among you. What I mean is this: One of you says, "I follow Paul"; another, "I follow Apollos"; another, "I follow Cephas"; still another, "I follow Christ."

Take note of the fact in both passages Paul uses language that implies the danger is already present, and not merely hypothetical.

Confront:

- Acts 13:9-10 Then Saul—also called Paul—filled with the Holy Spirit... said, "You son of the Devil, full of all deceit and all fraud, enemy of all righteousness! Won't you ever stop perverting the straight paths of the Lord?

- 1 Timothy 5:20 Publicly rebuke those who sin, so that the rest will also be afraid.

- Matthew 18:15-16 If your brother sins against you, go and rebuke him in private. If he listens to you, you have won your brother. But if he won't listen, take one or two more with you, so that by the testimony of two or three witnesses every fact may be established.

Avoid

- Romans 16:17 I appeal to you, brethren, take note of those who create dissentions and difficulties, in opposition to the doctrine which you have been taught. Avoid them.

- 2 Tim 2:16-17 Avoid such godless chatter, for it will lead people into more and more ungodliness, and their talk will eat its way like gangrene: such men are Hymenaeus and Philetus;

- Matthew 18:17 If he pays no attention to them, tell the church. But if he doesn't pay attention even to the church, let him be like an unbeliever and a tax collector to you.

Notice Paul calls these proven antagonists out by name! Although this flies in the face of the familiar adage, "If you can't say something nice, don't say anything at all," Scripture must trump human maxims.

The obvious question should be, "how can antagonists be identified?" Haugh identified 20 red flags, to which I (Rodney) have added one. This list, along with short descriptions of each behavior, should help you determine if antagonists are causing division in the church.

The **red flags** of antagonists are as follows

1. A previous track-record of antagonistic behavior. The bad-behavior experienced today is not new in the church. This person has acted antagonistically (see definition) in the past Thom Rainer notes some church members have actually been a part of several church splits. In other words, they have sown the

seeds of dissension in different congregations where they have been members.[16]

2. Parallel track-record... a track record of bad behavior outside of the church, in places such as home, hobbies and workplace.

3. The Nameless Other Flag... "there are lots who feel like me", "everyone feels you should resign." Antagonists love to make you feel outnumbered or out of touch.

4. The Instant Buddy: The first to take you to dinner, visit your office. If I could give this one "double points" I would. Antagonists want to immediately "befriend" the new pastor, committee chair or member.

5. The Predecessor-downer: *Denounce your predecessor* and *build you up* syndrome.

6. Gushing (and often premature) praise for your leadership. Saying things like, "you're the best Bible Study leader I've ever had" after one or two meetings.

7. Asking "I gotcha" questions: "What version of the Bible do real Christians use?" "What is the Bible's

---

[16] https://thomrainer.com/2015/03/nine-thoughts-church-splits/

position on Calvinism?" or "What is the church's position on eschatology?"

8. Overly Smooth and Charming: Be aware of wolves in sheep's clothing. As Proverbs 31:30 instructions, "Charm is deceitful."

9. The Church Hopper: "Finally, I found a church (or pastor) I can believe in."

10. Lies: Little lies common. Many antagonists lie about trivial matters, make up stories and distort the truth.

11. Aggressive methods: Over-the-top, unethical or combative means to get their voice heard.

12. The Flashing $$$ sign: Rich antagonists love this one and will threaten to withdraw financial support if they do not get their way.

13. The Note Taker: Take notes during pastoral visits, the coffee-hour or inappropriate times.

14. The Portfolio: Developing a "case" with "proof" of wrong-doings that shows evidence of a long-standing plan.

15. Cutting Comments: Saying things at times or places to cause great pain.

16. The Different Drummer: Always seeking to start new policies, change things or do it their own way.

17. The Pest: Always calling, emailing, posting or texting. *Take note: If they are always bothering you, they are bothering others!*

18. The Cause: Theological "isms", Politics, Home Schooling, KJV only...

19. The School of Hard Knocks: Little formal education but have gone through many struggles. Tend to brag about "their school."

20. The Poor Loser: When the church votes differently, the antagonists will get mad *and* get even.

21. Start at the Top: Disregard the "organizational chart and Matthew 18" and go straight to the top.

As I share with my students, "One red flag doth not an antagonist make." However, if you are seeing several red flags, you may be dealing with an antagonist.

Seven Steps for Dealing with Antagonists:
1) Pray for wisdom and guidance

2) Follow established policies and/or establish policies when and where needed.

3) Keep other church leaders informed: Have a confidant to talk to, such as your Mentor, Denomination Official, Director of Missions, another pastor, trusted deacon or elder.

4) Avoid abrupt changes—they tend to awaken antagonists.

5) Have a support group of Christian friends and peers.

6) Take control—the leader must set the agenda with the antagonist!

7) Prevention through the maintenance of an Anti-Antagonist Environment: Give an inch and they will take a mile. Keep them in check. An A-A Environment is facilitated by...
   a) A Good New Members Class
   b) Church Disciplines Policies in Place and Applied
   c) A Careful Review of the History of the Church
   d) Reading and Knowing the Church Documents
   e) Never making "Exceptions" to the Rules
   f) Following and Teaching Members in the Biblical process for Dealing with "Offences"
   g) Carefully accept new members who are not recommended by their former church (See Red Flag #1)

A word about those who were called to ministry...and said, "No" to the call or, for whatever reason, did not fulfill their calling. Over the years I have encountered several troublemakers in the church who were not antagonists, but forsook their calling:

A typical pattern for this category looks something like this:

- Believers called to be pastors become deacons
- Christians called as missionaries become church mission leaders
- Members called to Education Ministry become Sunday School Directors, etc....

While not everyone who forsakes the call becomes an antagonist or a divider, ignoring the signs can cause a great deal of conflict. Exploring the story of why the call was forsaken may provide a clear path forward in dealing with the issue.

Learning to discern those that are pretenders and antagonists takes some practice and grace. Getting to the heart issues of behavior is often complicated, but necessary if resolving conflict is the goal. Sometimes even cutting it off before it breaks out is the best prevention.

Discussion/application questions:

1) Based on the definitions in this chapter, can you identify someone in your past (or currently) that meets the criteria of an antagonist? If yes, how did it or does it impact the ministry?

2) What steps should be taken to deal with this antagonist?

3) Is there ever a time where church discipline or removal) would be in order? Why or why not?

4) Have you or are you currently recognizing a divider in ministry?

5) What steps should be taken?

6) Is there a possibility a person you know creating problems in the church is actually a case of an unfulfilled calling?

7) What steps should be taken?

12. The Personal Pain of Conflict

Even my close friend in whom I trusted, who ate my bread, has lifted his heel against me. Psalm 41:9

It is very difficult to be the pastor of your close friends. As a young minister, a well-meaning colleague advised a pastor should never make close friends with members from the church. This sad, but all too common attitude is not a biblical ideal but does reflect one of the personal challenge ministers and members face. Many times, pain, rejection, competition, and betrayal must be endured by those called to lead.

It is also difficult to maintain long-term relationships. I (Jeff) asked a crowd of over 3,500 people how many of them had great friends in High School. You know, the group you ran around with and believed you would always remain close friends. Almost every hand shot up. I asked how many people were still hanging out with the same group of people? Perhaps two hands were seen. Why?

"No good deed goes unpunished" is an endearing saying, which sadly, is also many times accurate. The pain of rejection is real. The heartbreak of betrayal cuts deep. These types of wounds can take a long time to fully heal, and even after the sting wears off, there probably will be a scar.

We learn at an early age to argue with those close to us. Most of us grew up around imperfect people and we know how selfish *those* people can be.

In fact, if we are honest, it is easier to argue and fuss with those we are closer to than with those that don't know us quite so well. With strangers and acquaintances, we tend to be more on guard than with family and close friends. We might be a bit more careful about what we say and how we say it than with those close to us.

That familiarity of relationship also opens us up to a deeper heartache and pain if fractured. In the church, we are surrounded by people that are supposed to be loving and filled with the fruit of the Spirit. We know most of us far fall short of this Biblical benchmark.

As two or more gather into the pursuit of some sort of ministry, relationships can become strained. Depending on the closeness of the people involved, the pain of the relationship ending can be devastating.

Even those who are not all that close to us relationally can unleash pain and heartache by speaking unkindly or assigning us wrong motives for our actions.

How do we walk through the pain of the following?

- Your best friend decides to quit attending your church.

- Your life long school chum begins to talk badly about you behind your back.
- Your lead elder you thought was on your side ends up leading a revolt against your leadership.
- Your young adult children leave your church to attend the new, on-fire, exciting one across town.
- You spend dozens of hours trying to help someone that later accuses you of not caring or doing anything to help.
- Your best friend decides to replace you with another best friend.

There are hundreds of other scenarios, but these are all too common in the church. While we would love for our church experience to be a wonderful time of floating around on a cloud in the Spirit, the truth is many times body life is messy, painful and full of disappointment.

We have many options when it comes to dealing with offenses, including overlooking them, learning from them and not repeating the same behavior towards others.

Offenses and hurts can also drive us to examine our motives, actions and attitudes that may have triggered a reaction from our friend. We are not perfect, and there may be some measure of truth in the painful accusations hurled at us. Even if there is only a small percentage of truth within the complaint, we would do well to deal with it.

Short of moving to a deserted island, we will encounter pain, heartache, and relational difficulties, so how do we deal with all of it? There is no perfect answer but a Perfect Savior who provides us great insight and we know He was uniquely acquainted with pain and suffering.

What follows is something that I (Jeff) wrote in another book of mine that might help us navigate through some of the pain in relationships.

It is inevitable hurts will come to us in this life, but sometimes they are over the top painful. A beloved spouse violates their marriage vows. A dearly loved child turns on you and curses you to your face. A friend, you believed was closer than a brother, is caught spreading lies and gossip about you. These situations, and dozens more like them, are real and they cause a great deal of tears and heartache.

I'm not denying the pain of these type circumstances, but I will challenge us to figure out a way to respond to them in love.

Jesus was betrayed by Judas, rejected by all the disciples, and Peter denied he even knew Him three times. All of these would have caused emotional pain and disappointment to the Savior, so, Jesus can relate to us in our pain of rejection perfectly.

> And the Lord turned and looked at Peter. And Peter remembered the saying of the Lord, how he had said to him, "Before the rooster crows today, you will deny me three times." Luke 22:61

Our bloodied, beaten Savior, when He needed the support of one of His best friends, was disappointed in the worst way. Can you imagine the look on Jesus' face at that precise moment of Peter's third denial?

My point is not an attempt to define what Jesus was thinking at that moment, but to guarantee you our Savior understood our relational pain.

> For because he himself has suffered when tempted, he is able to help those who are being tempted. Hebrews 2:18

> For we do not have a high priest who is unable to sympathize with our weaknesses, but one who in every respect has been tempted as we are, yet without sin. Hebrews 4:15

We know Jesus forgave those that crucified Him for while He was hanging on the cross, He cried out for their forgiveness. We also know Jesus went out of His way to restore Peter after the resurrection because John gives us the details of the process in John 21. Jesus asks Peter three times if he loves Him, and we know Peter finally says, "Lord you know everything, you know I do."

Jesus knows our pain because He suffered pain. Jesus knows what it is like to be tempted with anger, bitterness, and revenge, for He must have been to relate to us in our struggles as the writer of Hebrews shared with us. Jesus knows.

Jesus walked in forgiveness and so must we. Jesus forgave when those that hurt Him didn't deserve it or earn it and so must we. Jesus forgave others without them even asking for it and so must we.

Let me be perfectly clear, this is not easy, but it is required. Please carefully consider the following passages on the topic of forgiveness. If we read them slowly, prayerfully, and begin to understand the ramifications, they should send a shiver up our spines if we consider them deeply:

Give us this day our daily bread, and forgive us our debts, as we also have forgiven our debtors. And lead us not into temptation but deliver us from evil. For if you forgive others their trespasses, your heavenly Father will also forgive you, but if you do not forgive others their trespasses, neither will your Father forgive your trespasses.
Matthew 6:11-14

Do we really believe this passage? Jesus, while instructing His disciples in prayer, ties together provision, temptation *and* our Father's forgiveness to how we forgive those that have hurt, wounded, betrayed, or caused us pain.

Words like, "if" and "neither" should give us pause in this area of forgiveness. Yes, I know we are forgiven based on the blood of Jesus, yet, this passage nags at my mind and heart.

As does the story in Matthew 18. Most of us are familiar with the chapter and I mentioned it earlier. Church discipline is often the focus we see in this chapter, but Matthew chose elsewhere how to end the chapter.

The Parable of the Unforgiving Servant completes the chapter and it has a chilling ending:

So also, my heavenly Father will do to every one of you if you do not forgive your brother from your heart. Matthew 18:35

Do we believe this passage and what it implies? We know the story and are often upset with the wicked servant that refused to forgive someone that owed him a much smaller debt than he had just been forgiven, but do we make the application intended by Jesus?

"If we do not forgive our brother" should give us pause. Will God actually do the same thing to us if we fail to forgive? The passage certainly seems to say so. I am not proposing some new theology, simply urging we elevate the importance of forgiveness that Jesus clearly states in this parable.

> And whenever you stand praying, forgive, if you have anything against anyone, so that your Father also who is in heaven may forgive you your trespasses. Mark 11:25

Have you ever been praying, and God brings into your mind a face from your past? Perhaps you keep reliving a painful experience. Jesus instructs His disciples that when you are praying, and you realize you need to forgive someone, do so. Immediately. Why? "So that your Father in heaven may forgive you!" Are the two aspects of forgiveness really that connected in God's mind and ways? It would seem so.

I must let go to receive. It is difficult to receive something when my hands are closed. If I hold on to anger, hurt, bitterness, and my rights, it is hard to open my hands and heart to my loving, Heavenly Father's gifts of grace, mercy, forgiveness, and freedom. I can only hold so much at any time.

> Judge not, and you will not be judged; condemn not, and you will not be condemned; forgive, and you will be forgiven; Luke 6:37

We love the first part of this verse and even most unbelievers can quote it – judge not! However, the verse does not stop there. Forgiveness is also brought into the company of judging and condemning. Ouch. Does this mean if we don't forgive others, we won't be forgiven? Why would we take the chance? Forgive quickly as we have been forgiven.

> Put on then, as God's chosen ones, holy and beloved, compassionate hearts, kindness, humility, meekness, and patience, bearing with one another and, if one has a complaint against another, forgiving each other; as the Lord has forgiven you, so you also must forgive. And above all these put on love, which binds everything together in perfect harmony.
> Colossians 3:12-14

Paul states clearly if we have a complaint against anyone (and who does not?), we must forgive. How can we? Because the Lord has forgiven us, we must forgive.

What about those that hate us?

"If you love those who love you, what benefit is that to you? For even sinners love those who love them. And if you do good to those who do good to you, what benefit is that to you? For even sinners do the same. And if you lend to those from whom you expect to receive, what credit is that to you? Even sinners lend to sinners, to get back the same amount. But love your enemies, and do good, and lend, expecting nothing in return, and your reward will be great, and you will be sons of the Most

High, for he is kind to the ungrateful and the evil. Be merciful, even as your Father is merciful. Luke 6:32-36

There are other verses, but these are sufficient to at least make us consider the benefits and problems centering around forgiveness.

If we hope to grow to where we can love those who hurt us, we must begin with forgiveness. We must learn to release others from our pain.

Some of us remember the cameras that took a picture that then came out of the front of the

> This is natural but certainly not godly.

device. The picture would take a few minutes to become clear and we would marvel at the technology.

When someone hurts us deeply the temptation is to lock them into a snapshot. We take their face and freeze-frame it in the worst possible fashion and place it a deep place in our heart.

Every so often we take the photo out of our hearts and scream at it, maybe curse it, and speak all manner of evil against it. We relive the pain, hurt, words, and experience over and over again. In short, we have not forgiven the person that violated us. This is natural but certainly not godly.

If we are to freely receive God's forgiveness for our huge debt of sin, we must release those that hurt us from this dungeon of bitterness we keep them in. We have grown and changed over the years, and perhaps the culprit has as well. Even if they have not, we have been freely forgiven and according to all those verses we just read, we must forgive. We have no choice.

If we refuse, our destination is one of bitterness and guilt. The writer of Hebrews is clear:

> See to it that no one fails to obtain the grace of God; that no "root of bitterness" springs up and causes trouble, and by it many become defiled;
> Hebrews 12:15

Bitterness does not help anyone, and it certainly does not hurt the one that wounded us. In fact, they are rarely aware of our bitterness towards them. The old saying goes something like, "we drink poison thinking we are hurting the other person." How foolish.

One way to avoid becoming bitter is to move quickly to forgiveness. Release people to the hand of the Lord. God is more than capable of protecting your reputation, seeing the guilty are punished, and bringing about justice. We must forgive so we can be forgiven.

The previous section was taken from a book entitled; *Love in the Face of Life*, and I simply do not know any other way to get to the other side of pain and disappointment than through love and forgiveness.

In *Pastoral Helmsmanship*, I (Rodney) tell the story of how love and forgiveness were the tools God used to bring healing and purpose following my daughter's experience of being sexually abused by a church member. Obedience may not be easy, nor is it natural, however, one cannot experience spiritual growth when we harbor unforgiveness and refuse to love those who harm us.

Relationships can bring great joy as well as deep pain. How we go through it will determine whether we remain effective for the Kingdom or sidelined by hurts, wounds and bitterness. I pray we follow our Lord's example and complete the work of loving others we are clearly assigned by our Lord and Savior Jesus.

Discussion/application questions:

1) Take enough time to pray, in solitude, and ask the Lord if there are those whom you need to forgive.
2) Reflect on a time when someone forgave you. How did their forgiveness impact the relationship?
3) As the Holy Spirit brings people to mind, ask the Lord how to deal with the pain, the hurt and ultimately how to forgive. It may take several times praying and reading through the Scriptures. Stay with it until God gives you a release.
4) As you periodically revisit this topic, continue to seek God and He will lead you where you need to go.

13. Multiplication by Division

And there arose a sharp disagreement, so that they separated from each other. Barnabas took Mark with him and sailed away to Cyprus, but Paul chose Silas and departed, having been commended by the brothers to the grace of the Lord. Acts 15:39-40

God works in strange ways. In the verses above Paul and Barnabas have an intense fight over Mark. Whoever was at fault, and however it ended, a split happened. While we don't know all that happened, we do know God redeemed the situation years later. As will be explained in the next chapter, Paul later requested for Mark to come join him and Silas. For now, let us focus on the fact God used a split to further His work and Kingdom.

The truth is sometimes leaving is the correct thing to do. Even when we do not leave properly, God's ability to work everything out for good (Romans 8:28) remains. With God there is no helpless situation.

In past generations, the prevailing attitude towards church splits was like divorce among church members—something shameful, unbiblical and to be avoided at all cost. This attitude afforded little grace.

My (Rodney) own attitude towards church splits began to change after hearing Phil Langley, who was at that time my supervisor with the California Baptist Convention, share his observation that many splits were "churches that were pregnant and did not know it."

Langley's perspective was one that believed some church splits had the potential to result in two vibrant congregations. Around the same time, Dan Reiland, a missiologist who worked with John Maxwell, wrote the often-quoted statement, "A Church Split is a poorly handled church-planting project." Langley and Reiland helped me to see church splits from a Romans 8:28 perspective.

What does it take for "good" to come from a church split? The starting point for the congregation and leadership is to engage in a sober review of the likelihood for health and healing. Without intervention, my observation is many, if not most, splits die in the first five years.

Unquestionably, some congregations birthed from a split hang on tenaciously for years, decades and longer. But over the course of time, only a few thrive. Most splits succumb to spiritual impotency or death as the cancer of the split eats away at the health of the body.

Over the course of four decades, I (Rodney) have conducted dozens of churches "autopsies." The cause of death (closure) is often rooted in the issue that caused the split. For many splits, the negative community impact for the split and the splinter is great and enduring.

When interviewing community members near a church that split, merchants and residents often say things such as, "Oh that's the church that fought all the time until it split."

In most church splits the flashpoint for the split is the pastor. In some cases, the pastor is clearly the problem. In others, the pastor is simply a convenient and visible scapegoat. These are the leaders I mourn for, as most pastors (and spouses) who have been through a church split will bear the scars from the experience for the rest of their ministries.

Church splits typically originate within power groups that exist in the church. The power group may be a formal body, such as deacons or elders, or an informal group that wields power or influence in the church.

Some church members have been a part of several church splits. In other words, they have sown the seeds of dissension in different congregations where they have been members or have been part of multiple splits within one congregation.

Therefore, be cautious about accepting new members who are not vetted by their former church. Problem church members tend to recycle. While serving in a small county seat town of under 1,500 people, I was surprised to find five churches of the same denomination. Four were splits from the original church, all within a period of 75 years.

Church splits are typically preceded by inactive church members becoming active members. It is amazing to attend a church business meeting or conference where divisive issues are discussed. Inactive members seem to come out of the woodwork for these meetings.

As the conflict spreads, recruitment efforts intensify. While serving with a church in conflict, one staff member told me he was, "starting to go door-to-door among inactive members to win people who would side with the pastor." My only solace was the staff member was not a graduate of the seminary where I teach.

> **There are often no winners in church splits.**

Church splits are more likely to occur in "country club" churches. A country club church is a metaphor for a church where many of the members have a sense of entitlement instead of an attitude of service. They pay their "dues" to get their way. And if they don't get their way on every issue, even minor issues, they may sow the seeds of dissension that lead to a church split.

Some churches still split over doctrinal issues. Although doctrinal church splits are not as common as other splits, they still take place. Whereas doctrinal splits were common among mainline churches in the previous century, they are becoming more frequent among evangelical churches today.

Other churches split over financial issues. These issues include disagreements over budget priorities, mission expenditures, incurring of debt, facility expenditures, and building programs.

There are often no winners in church splits. Those who leave are typically hurt and angry. Those who stay tend to experience the pain and frustration that stems a steady, if not steep, rate of decline in attendance and, eventually, finances. Added to these declines is a reputation in the community that is damaged significantly—and sometimes permanently.

The Etiology of a Split

Church splits often result from personal convictions or expectations. Differences in opinion regarding a pastor, polity or finances can led to disagreements strong enough to fracture the church. In these cases, there is little or no animosity or underlying sin at the root of the conflict. An example of this type of conflict is recorded in Acts 15:37-39, as was briefly touched upon in the opening of this chapter.

Barnabas wanted to take along John Mark. But Paul insisted they should not take along this man who had deserted them in Pamphylia and had not gone on with them to the work. They had such a sharp disagreement they parted company, and Barnabas took Mark with him and sailed off to Cyprus.

On a positive note, it appears two mission teams rather than one resulted from the split. Paul and Silas embark on what becomes the Second Missionary Journey (Acts 15:36-18:22), while Barnabas and Mark head to Cyprus. We also know John Mark and Paul were likely reconciled later (2 Timothy 4:11).

On a sadder note, we learn of what might be a residual effect of the split in Galatians 2:13, where we read, "And the rest of the Jews acted hypocritically along with him, with the result that even Barnabas was carried away by their hypocrisy." Even today, church splits resulting from personal convictions or expectations can result in conflicts severe enough to lead to members of a congregation going separate ways.

Church splits can arise when a church starts to drift from biblical moorings. On a grand scale, the Protestant Reformation was a church split arising from a replacement of biblical orthodoxy and qualified leadership for tradition and political maneuvering. Although Martin Luther pursued restoration before reformation, his concerns were passed over, and he was rejected as a heretic. In a similar way, the only recourse for some churches is to start anew.

Dan Reiland writes, "There is a fine line between a church split and a church plant in terms of outcome." Tom Cheyney affirms this fine line by calling some splits a "splate" --a split that becomes a plant. Liberty University co-founder Elmer Towns notes several conditions when a church split is justified.

1. New members are not being saved and baptized.
2. When doctrine has been compromised
3. When a church permits obvious sin that keeps the church from fulfilling its purpose

When conflict and disagreements arise from conditions or doctrinal matters that are justified, splits are not evil or ill advised. Nor are they destined for failure.

During one of the many conferences I attended as a church planting missionary, I recall hearing a speaker say church splits were more likely to succeed than church plants. Although I cannot validate this statement with facts and figures, I am not surprised. Many church splits start with "uneducated enthusiasm" which is in stark contrast to those planted.

As a case-in-point to this last statement, one

denomination reports 4 out of 5 new churches will fail, and only 1 in 10 sustain at larger than 100 people in worship.[17] I would venture to say the viability rate of church splits is higher than 4 out of 5.

Consider the following. Leaders of what Elmer Towns classifies as a justified church split are often zealous, thus they are likely to be financially and physically invested in the endeavor. Added to zealousness, members often bring years of experience to the new church.

Towns identifies four strategic advantages to new churches started as splits:

1. Church has firm financial commitments
2. Church has a core of people
3. Church has committed and mature believers
4. Church is closely knit around a cause

He also points out several potential disadvantages:

1. Usually they have a poor reputation in the community and among other churches.
2. Bitterness may hinder its ministry.
3. The new church may be established for some other reason than evangelism.
4. People who could not get along with others in the old church will cause problems in the new church.
5. Strong opposition from old church.[18]

---

[17] Evangelical Friends Church, 9 Myths About Church Planting, https://efcmaym.org/ministries/church-planting/9-myths-about-church-planting/, accessed April 1, 2019. It should be noted that this article also shows that well-conceived church plants have an 86% success rate after 4 years.

[18] Elmer Towns, Getting a Church Started, 3rd ed. (Lynchburg, VA, Liberty University, 1993), 75.

As I noted in *Spinoff Churches*, a healthy church willing to take a split under its wings can alleviate or reduce potentials disadvantages, such as poor reputation in the community.[19]

In much the same way a marriage prior to the birth of a child reduces the stigma caused by an out of wedlock pregnancy, a healthy sponsoring church can help a new church weather the pain of a split. Please note the pain is not eliminated, nor is any sin that led to the split being condoned.

Adopting a Church Split

One of the most loving ways to deal with unplanned pregnancies is through adoption. Adoption is more than just "taking a church under its wings." Adoption involves placing a group that has split for a justifiable reason and sponsoring them as a church plant, thus providing legal, financial and material support.

Adoption clearly associates the church split with the parent church and provides a healthy environment for the split to heal, mature and thrive. Be forewarned, always think twice (and pray more) before adopting a split that is not justified or utilized ungodly means during the fight. To do this, leaders from the adopting church must get the whole story.

In the book of Esther, a clear contrast between Haman and Mordeci appears. When Haman tells the King about

---

[19] Rodney Harrison, Tom Cheyney, Don Overstreet, Spin-Off Churches (Nashville, TN, Broadman & Holman, 2007), 104.

Mordeci, he gives Ahasuerus less than the whole story and implies all Jews are disloyal subjects—omitting or ignoring key truths in his story, including Mordeci's actions recorded in Esther 2:22-23, in which he saves the king's life. In contrast to these half-truths, Mordeci is keen to establish the whole story, along with supporting documentation as recorded in Esther 4:6-9.

Seasoned ministry leaders are not surprised that Paul includes gossips in the list of vile sinners (Romans 1:29-31). Unchecked, gossip will ruin a church.

Truth is the best weapon against gossip, so be sure to have the information required to make an informed decision. Therefore, prior to adopting a church split, leaders should seek to interview members from both sides of the conflict. Gaining a clear picture of the issues will help validate whether the split was justifiable.

If the interview process results in greater confusion, that might be a good indicator that adoption of the split is ill-advised. It is also important to recognize the networks of relationships that permeate the split and splinter. In all likelihood, your church has members who conduct business or go to school with families involved in both sides of the split. Once word gets out your church is adopting a split, these relationships may be impacted.

Ironically, after a split, many in the new splinter group will maintain friendships with those from the church. These networks are a perplexing reality and are similar to dysfunctional families in that it is difficult to make heads or tails of the allegiances among these members.

Next Steps:
If you are part of a church split, consider the following:

1. Establishing a relationship with an existing healthy church that will either take the church split under their wings as a partner in ministry or adopt the split as a church plant.

2. Financial support may be needed to rent a facility or purchase property. Beyond that, in many ways, a church split's needs are similar to those experienced by a family that has experienced a divorce...things that one assumes will be there are suddenly gone. Office equipment, serving sets for the Lord's Supper, a baptistery, sound system, worship instruments, seating and pulpits are often high on the list of felt needs for these new churches. By helping the new church acquire these things through short or long-term loans or gifts, the sponsoring church can tangibly assist the new congregations.

3. The new church may benefit from the "covering" provided by sponsorship. The sponsoring church can assist the new work by providing liability insurance and bringing them under the constitution and by-laws of the sponsoring church until such time the new church constitutes.

4. Many churches birthed as splits will benefit from a healthy role model. Involving members in the new church in activities that model church health and vitality may serve the dual purpose of building bridges between the two congregations and provide ministry opportunities that are beyond the capability of the new church.

5. Help the new church to extend the "right hand of fellowship" to other local pastors, churches and denominational leaders. As the sponsoring church, you are providing legitimacy to the new church birthed out of a split as well as introducing the new church leaders to your "network" of relationships and resources. Sometimes a simple call to a respected pastor or area leader inviting them to lunch with the new church leaders can provided untold good.

It may help churches and individuals to recall that just about every denomination in existence arose out of a split. Remember, Christianity was considered nothing more than a split off Judaism. Often, God births something new to take us were we would not go otherwise.

Just as Paul came to recognize John Mark as a valuable member of his team, the split may result in a valuable new church in God's field.

Discussion/Application Questions:

1) If you have ever lived through a church-split describe your perspective of what took place. Who was at fault and how could have it been prevented?

2) Even though there are not winners in a church split, how can God redeem these situations for His glory? Explain.

3) How could "adopting a church split" work to limit the damage caused by a split among the membership and community

4) How does forgiveness play into the church split? Explain your answer.

14. When is Enough, Enough?

I still had no peace of mind, because I did not find my brother Titus there. So, I said goodbye to them and went on to Macedonia. 2 Corinthians 2:13

There is a time to call it quits. Some relationships are toxic and need to be stopped. This happens at a personal and at a church level.

As we contemplate how to walk through conflict, there is an appropriate time to avoid it completely. Perhaps staying and fighting through will cause too much relational damage. Maybe the issue is beyond resolving.

Paul reveals this possibility in Romans 12:18 - *If it is possible, as far as it depends on you, live at peace with everyone.* What is not stated, but clearly implied is sometimes it simply is not possible. It takes two to work through conflict and sometimes others are not ready or willing to do so.

One issue God will have to deal with shortly after our arrival in the next life is all the unresolved relational damage we left behind. Brothers and sisters unable to resolve their differences in the temporal life, must and will be able to do so in the eternal one. How could we live in an eternal state of arguing, unresolved hurts and offenses?

While I don't pretend to understand how God will do it, I know He must. Eternity will be a place without pain, sorrow and tears. Perhaps we simply will gain enough insight to understand what was really going on and those issues will no longer matter. Maybe God will simply pour out enough grace that we can't remember the offenses. Whatever He does to solve the issue, it will be perfect, but it must be solved.

We are not in the next life yet, so we must learn how to deal with conflicts, relational damage, offenses, and such now.

While breaking a relationship may seem like a failure at the time, perhaps it simply is an attempt to redeem it from another direction. Maybe some time needs to pass to allow time to heal, gain a new perspective, or allow the Holy Spirit to bring clarity and healing to the situation.

If constant arguing, disagreements, anger, and wounds keep arising from being together, then the option to leave is always a possibility. Of course, this understanding must be tempered with marriage and other legal or covenantal agreements. We simply don't walk away from our marriage partner because we argue, or we don't violate our word in an agreement because of difficulties. In these cases, there is a higher law and principle at work.

Let me give a clarification point here, we need not stay in an abusive situation just to show love to someone. Unless we are being persecuted for our faith in Jesus, I don't find any verses in the Scripture that endorse abuse, or the submitting to it. If you are living with someone that is abusing you, leave, and do it now.

If that person is your spouse, I am not necessarily advocating divorce, but you do not have to stay in that situation. Seek Biblical counsel and get help. Now. Today.

If that person is a family member and you are being abused, tell someone today. Now. Right now. You are not showing love to that person by submitting to abuse. In fact, you are hurting them and not loving them. Sin loves the darkness and hates being exposed.

By your silence and acceptance of their behavior, you are reinforcing the rightness of the deeds in their mind. That is not helpful or loving and is encouraging them to continue their sinful behavior. The most loving thing you could possibly do is expose it, not live with it or cover it over.

While not breaking legal contracts or marriages, we are referring to leaving a church, stepping down from a position, quitting a job, or breaking away from an unhealthy personal relationship and whether that is ever an option.

We have looked at staff and board relationships in a previous chapter, so I would refer you to those for gaining understanding in how to function in those relationships. However, even in these type relationships, there may come a time when it is in everyone's best interest to walk away, rather than stay and remain in conflict.

If a situation becomes untenable, unredeemable, is causing damage to others, destroying your family, or bringing potential damage to the Body of Christ, it might be time to consider removing yourself from the situation.

This does not mean there will never be a time to revisit these relationships, but perhaps now is not that time. For the sake of unity, personal wellbeing, and protecting the reputation of Christ and others, it might be time to gracefully leave.

These are not righteous motives.

If it becomes clear it is time to leave, then please do so in the most gracious, least divisive way possible. The temptation is to rally others to our cause, make sure everyone understands just how innocent we are, and to show how the others really are to blame. These are not righteous motives and could lead to a church split as discussed in the previous chapter.

If it becomes apparent it is time to step down from serving in a leadership position, then go privately to the leader(s) and let them know the reasons for your decision. Ask them if there are any unresolved offenses you can attempt to make right, and then leave quietly. You do not want to be guilty of spreading strife, division, and death within the Body of Christ, nor do you want to leave with debts owed.

Samuel's words are a good principle to consider:

> Here I am; testify against me before the Lord and before his anointed. Whose ox have I taken? Or whose donkey have I taken? Or whom have I defrauded? Whom have I oppressed? Or from whose hand have I taken a bribe to blind my eyes with it? Testify against me and I will restore it to you."
> 1Samuel 12:3

When we walk away from a relationship it is often best not to burn the bridge through gossip, slander, self-justification and bitterness. You never know what God will do in your life or in theirs. Our God is redemptive and loving. We would be wise to be the same.

Most of us are familiar with the story of Paul and Barnabas shared throughout the book of Acts and used in other places in this book. Before his dramatic conversion, Saul, later to change his name to Paul, was a scary man. Empowered with letters from the religious rulers, Saul was "ravishing" the church and the believers.

> But Saul, still breathing threats and murder against the disciples of the Lord, went to the high priest 2 and asked him for letters to the synagogues at Damascus, so that if he found any belonging to the Way, men or women, he might bring them bound to Jerusalem. Acts 9:1-2

Barnabas, also known as the Son of Encouragement, takes Saul the new covert under his wings and vouches for him. Quite a relationship risk! They travel together and even begin to disciple another young man named Mark.

For whatever reason, Mark leaves the trio in the middle of a trip and Paul doesn't seem to care much for it. Later, when Barnabas asks to bring young Mark along, Paul wants no part of it. Two servants, two good men, one nasty argument.

> Now Barnabas wanted to take with them John called Mark. But Paul thought best not to take with them one who had withdrawn from them in Pamphylia and had not gone with them to the work. And there arose a sharp disagreement, so

that they separated from each other. Barnabas took Mark with him and sailed away to Cyprus, but Paul chose Silas and departed, having been commended by the brothers to the grace of the Lord. Acts 15:37-40

How do you not get along with a guy named, "The Son of Encouragement?" The point of this is not to determine guilt but to see sometimes good, godly people, even those that are spiritual heavyweights can and do separate.

We also know Mark was still used of God because he became one of Peter's right-hand men. And, we know even later in life Paul requested Mark be sent for.

Luke alone is with me. Get Mark and bring him with you, for he is very useful to me for ministry. 2 Timothy 4:11

It may be necessary to leave a relationship for a season. Perhaps there will be a time in the future where that friendship, working partnership, or family bond can be restored.

Some other considerations regarding leaving relationships include having friendships that are healthy and lead us into maturity not into sin or carnality.

Whoever walks with the wise becomes wise, but the companion of fools will suffer harm. Proverbs 13:20

The one who keeps the law is a son with understanding, but a companion of gluttons shames his father. Proverbs 28:7

He who loves wisdom makes his father glad, but a companion of prostitutes squanders his wealth. Proverbs 29:3

"You win or lose by the friends you choose," was a sentence from a children's song we used to quote quite a bit when our children were young. It is a true thought. Friends will lead us somewhere and we need to be wise about the destination.

One other thought about saying "enough", or at least being wise in our relationships; many end up experiencing sexual immorality due to simply being unwise. Paul's words are clear:

Flee from sexual immorality. Every other sin a person commits is outside the body, but the sexually immoral person sins against his own body. 1 Corinthians 6:18

Sometimes we are told to stand and fight and, in this case, we are told to run away! There are times when saying no to a relationship is wiser than saying yes. David, Solomon, and a host of others have fallen prey to sexual immorality and sometimes we must walk away from disaster before we end up with a huge amount of regret.

We need to operate in love with wisdom. Sometimes relationships need to end and at other times they need to be put on hold. If love guides us and we learn to listen to those around us we can avoid disasters.

We will have relationship failures because we are human, but we can learn from them, strive not to repeat them and share what we have learned with others. Nothing is wasted in the Kingdom if we allow God to redeem us!

If you are considering leaving a church, breaking off a relationship or find yourself in the midst of a difficult one, then seek counsel. Seek the Lord for His perfect timing and empowering grace and let 1 Corinthians 13:4-7 be your guide.

Discussion/Application Questions:

1) Have you ever been part of a toxic relationship? How did you resolve it?
2) How would you describe the best possible way to leave a church?
3) What does "don't burn your bridges" mean and how do we not light the fire to do so?
4) Why does the Scripture say to stay and fight sometimes and at other times tell us to run?
5) How can God redeem broken relationships?

15. Personal vs. Kingdom Agendas

But seek first his kingdom and his righteousness, and all these things will be given to you as well. Matthew 6:33

As my (Rodney) wife was reviewing the menu for our annual Easter Sunday family gathering, she said, "What about green bean hot dish?" My response was a quick and decisive, "No." At that point my wife reminded me, "You know, just because you don't like green bean hot dish does not mean others might not enjoy it." Guilty as charged. My personal preference had become a personal agenda. When personal preferences become agendas, the Body of Christ suffers. At a minimum, the offender is communicating the message, "my preferences outweigh your preferences." A Kingdom agenda puts aside personal preferences for the mission of the church and the advancement of the Kingdom.

One of the marks of the Spirit controlled believer is the willingness to "submit to one another out of reverence for

Christ" (Ephesians 5:21). Paul illustrates this in his letter to the Corinthians when he writes:

> Food will not commend us to God. We are no worse off if we do not eat, and no better off if we do. But take care that this right of yours does not somehow become a stumbling block to the weak. For if anyone sees you who have knowledge eating in an idol's temple, will he not be encouraged, if his conscience is weak, to eat food offered to idols? And so, by your knowledge this weak person is destroyed, the brother for whom Christ died. Thus, sinning against your brothers and wounding their conscience when it is weak, you sin against Christ. Therefore, if food makes my brother stumble, I will never eat meat, lest I make my brother stumble (1 Corinthians 8:8-13).

In Paul's illustration, some in the church may have felt buying meat sacrificed to idols at the pagan temples was a matter of good stewardship, as it cost less than meat from other sources. Others in the church would associate this meat with pagan worship, and knowingly eating such meat was a matter of spiritual compromise. In Romans 14:1 Paul implies it is the responsibly of those maturing in the faith to ensure personal preferences do not hijack Kingdom outcomes. Towards the end of this discourse, Paul instructs, "So then let us pursue what makes for peace and for mutual upbuilding (Romans 14:19).

The list of contemporary personal vs. Kingdom agendas will not likely include food sacrificed to idols. Today, the agenda issues are more likely to involve music and worship preferences, worship times, use of technology, budget priorities and pot-luck vs. catered fellowship meal preferences. Unless we are intentional in our reflection and honest in our self-evaluation, we can quickly and decisively put our personal agenda above the Kingdom agenda.

We all have an ego and we all have pride. Some display it more readily than others, but who can claim to be perfect in these two? Serving in the ministry can be very ego stroking. Compliments often flow, and many younger believers sometimes idolize their leaders. We know that is foolish, but still, sometimes it goes to our heads.

Jesus' words were clear about what it is we should be seeking and whose Kingdom it is. It is God's, not ours.
The Church is Jesus' and not ours. Jesus said He would build His Church and the gates of hell would not overcome it (Matthew 16:18). We are under shepherds that serve the Great Shepherd and if we get this order reversed, we are wrong.

Being called to service in the Kingdom is just that - service. If we forget this underlying principle, then we need to return to our example in John 13:3-5.

> Jesus, knowing that the Father had given all things into his hands, and that he had come from God and was going back to God, rose from supper.

If we didn't already know the rest of the text we could stop here and guess what Jesus was going to do next. Perhaps it would be good to place ourselves in this picture and ask what we would do at this moment. Or perhaps, try to get into the disciple's mind for a moment and wonder what they thought Jesus would do next. Based on the reaction of the disciples, and especially Peter in this chapter, we know they were shocked.

Perhaps they thought Jesus was going to give them some explanation of the greatness of the Kingdom, and if they did, they would not be far off. Jesus knew He had all authority and that He came from God and was soon to be reunited with Him in heaven. That would probably lead many of us onto a wild ego trip.

We do know the rest of the story, and we know what Jesus did.

> He laid aside his outer garments, and taking a towel, tied it around his waist. Then he poured water into a basin and began to wash the disciples' feet and to wipe them with the towel that was wrapped around him.

Jesus served His disciples by performing the lowliest task possible. While the disciples were arguing about which one of them would ultimately be the greatest, the Greatest One possible showed them how to lead. We would be wise to contemplate this section of Scripture often.

Jesus offered this explanation to His perplexed disciples in John 13:12-14:

> When he had washed their feet and put on his outer garments and resumed his place, he said to them, "Do you understand what I have done to you? You call me Teacher and Lord, and you are right, for so I am. If I then, your Lord and Teacher, have washed your feet, you also ought to wash one another's feet. For I have given you an example, that you also should do just as I have done to you.

The old song is true - "If you want to be great in the Kingdom, learn to be a servant of all." If we miss this critical point, we, and those under our care, will suffer. God has called His leaders to be servants.

This should bring some questions to our mind:

- Whose kingdom are we building?
- Whose should we be?
- How do we know?
- What do we do if we are building incorrectly?
- What is the ultimate purpose of what we are doing?

There are of course other questions, but we certainly can't ignore these if we want to be effective in our ministry.

Tying this general concept back into a book on conflict should be obvious. We must ask ourselves how much of the conflict in our lives is directly tied back to building the wrong kingdom. How much of the strife, division, heartache and frustration is God allowing to remain in our lives due to having the wrong attitude, heart motives, or goal? We must answer these questions if we hope to grow, mature, and be effective in dealing with conflict.

Are we a servant? Are we willing to lay down our egos and do the most menial tasks for the sake of others? Jesus was and did.

Do we care about God's Kingdom first and foremost or is it about your reputation, goals, dreams and desires? Do we demand to receive the credit for what we do, or do we realize almost everything good that happens is because of others?

Are you a good planner? How do you think you became one? Excellent speaker? Who taught you, gave you grace for it, allowed you time to prepare, or makes sure you have a working microphone? Who captures it and produces it, so the wonderful message can be heard by others? Who inspired you?

The truth is we all stand on the shoulders of those who went before us. We all have those that help us, serve us, and make whatever we do possible. None of us would be anything without multiple others giving of themselves. This is true of other people, and it is certainly true of the grace of God which enables us to do whatever we achieve. If we ever lose sight of this, we are heading for a fall.

We must remember we are called to servant leadership. People are not a tool to be used to achieve an end goal. People are the goal. Buildings, programs and everything temporal will not last. Relationships and the investment we make in people will continue for eternity. We must choose wisely.

Discussion/Application Questions:

1) When have you observed a personal agenda take priority over a Kingdom agenda? What was the outcome?
2) How does seeking first the Kingdom of God work in real life?
3) How does living a life of service and leadership work in daily practice?
4) What would be a modern-day equivalent of foot washing?
5) Looking over your current giftings and skill set, who helped you along the way?
6) What does it mean to you when we say, "people are the goal?"

16. Embrace Grace

Proverbs 13:12 - Hope deferred makes the heart sick, but a desire fulfilled is a tree of life.

While most of us do not enjoy or look forward to conflict with others, we hope some enlightening and encouraging thoughts have been presented. Not all conflict is bad and sometimes it can be constructive.

While conflict is inevitable it does not have to be destructive and if we are people of faith, it does not have to be the final word in all situations.

God's Word is clear regarding love, unity and learning how to show a lost and dying world His people can learn to get along with each other.

There is power in unity and that is where God's blessing is commanded in Psalm 133:

> Behold, how good and pleasant it is when brothers dwell in unity! It is like the precious oil on the head, running down on the beard, on the beard of Aaron, running down on the collar of his robes! It is like the dew of Hermon, which falls on the mountains of Zion! For there the Lord has commanded the blessing, life forevermore.

The Psalmist knew what we will discover is walking in unity is a blessing of life. Unity is worth fighting for and seeking for life is the natural outworking of the process.

Not only is unity a natural byproduct of learning how to walk together through conflict, but personal growth will follow as well.

If we learn what our conflict management style is, and how we deal with differing personality types, and if we seek to walk in love towards others, laying down our selfish desires for unity, we will grow.

We all have verses in the Bible that resonate with us deeply. Mine (Jeff) is this one - Proverbs 27:17 - Iron sharpens iron, and one man sharpens another.

Through relationship difficulties over the years, growth has come into my life. When two pieces of iron clang together, sparks often fly. Little pieces of heated metal are knocked off and the result is sharper blades.

Through marriage, parenting, pastoring, shopping and even driving, little bits of myself have been knocked off through interaction with others. This is a good thing for there is much of the flesh that needs to be pared down through conflict.

As we learn to walk through conflict we will mature into useful tools in the Master's hands and that is always an excellent goal to desire.

Conflict can arise as discipline from our Lord, but we know the writer of Hebrews had excellent words to share with us on that topic:

Hebrews 12:11 - For the moment all discipline seems painful rather than pleasant, but later it yields the peaceful fruit of righteousness to those who have been trained by it.

We all probably desire peaceful fruit and that often arrives after a season of turmoil, conflict and then resolution leading to an outpouring of God's grace on all involved. That end is well worth the process!

Rarely do we grow during the easy, good times but we often grow strong under the pressure and pain of relationship turmoil. Therefore, it is well worth the effort to keep on praying, struggling, and learning to walk through the trials of conflict to reach the goal of growth.

Glenn's Final Thoughts:

I can never remember a time when I went through conflict where it was fun, pretty or easy. I do recall numerous incidences where God used it to shape me, grow me and ultimately help others in the process.

We must keep in mind God's big plan for our lives, and not focus on the need to get out of or avoid altogether the short-term pain that often accompanies dysfunctional conflict.

I remember a conflict that arose between a neighboring business regarding a business property I owned. He made all kinds of claims against our business, blocked our back exit with an immovable trash dumpster, called the local police on us on a regular basis with false violations, all because he found out one of his tenants was moving to one of our rental spaces.

He had a strong reputation in the community for being a slum lord and being an oppressive neighbor. I remember gathering evidence, taking pictures, hiring civil engineers, and spending many sleepless nights plotting and planning how I was going to not only prevail, but put this bully in his place.

Then a friend of mine suggested before I file a suite or do this person bodily harm, I might want to visit with an attorney friend of his. So, I gathered all my evidence and went to see the attorney. I first gave an overview of the problem, and then when I was about to pull out the mountain of evidence in my favor, he asked me a question. He said, "Are you are believer?" I said proudly "Well yes I am!" He then asked me a question: "Would you be open to me talking with you as a brother in Christ?" And I of course said "Sure." I had no idea what I had just signed up for.

He asked me a question I have repeated to others dozens and dozens of times. He said "Glenn, if you were able to remove yourself from this situation, and fast forward ten years, when you look back, how do you want the storyline to read?"

At that point I am thinking "Really? We are here to "get this bad guy" not create story lines!" He went on to share things about his practice he had learned over the years about divorces, lawsuits, harming people and lack of forgiveness. Whatever he said, I began to listen.

Before I could show him all the evidence that I had, he said to me "You need to go and apologize to your neighbor." I could NOT believe what he just said. I did nothing wrong, he is in the wrong, he is the known bully and you want ME to apologize to HIM???? I asked, "For what?" He said, "I don't know, but you need to go and apologize."

At that point I was in a spiritual daze. I did not know what to say. He told me to go back to my office and think about it, and if I still wanted to wage war, he would help.

After the brief 15-minute discussion, I went back to my car and just sat and cried like I had never cried before. I was devastated. I knew that God had spoken through this attorney, but I didn't understand everything. But I didn't have to. I just had to obey.

I called the neighbor and asked for an appointment. I walked into his office and he began the conversation with an incredibly smug look and feel. "Well son, it's not a bad thing to get in over your head." I REALLY wanted to hurt him.

With perhaps the greatest emotional pain suffered to date, I humbly apologized for taking his tenant and asked for his forgiveness. He emotionally and in a condescending manner patted me on my head and sent me back to my building. I was so embarrassed and humiliated. But I did however know I had no choice but to be obedient.

He then took the next step to add to my humiliation and blocked me from expanding into some desperately needed parking spaces. He said, and I quote "You will never get access to those spaces, unless over my dead body!" More abuse, more humiliation. I did not know when it would end. I did occasionally ask God "What is this all about?"

Six months later, at age 55, he passed away, I suspect bitter and lonely. We waited another six months before approaching his wife about the spaces we needed, and she said her husband would never have allowed it. A few short months later she passed away, she was in her mid-40s.

We did finally get access to that much needed real state to help grow our work with churches, but know I was shocked by both events and would never have wished any harm to either of them. I am also quick to point out there was no justice in what happened and no satisfaction, perhaps just a sense of wonderment and peace.

What I did take away is God is in control, in the short run and the long run, even when we don't understand. Seek God in all conflict, and perhaps heed the advice of my attorney friend and think about the story you want written in eternity when looking back at your life.

Rodney's Final Thoughts:

In Galatians 5, the deeds of the flesh are evident in acts of immorality, impurity, sensuality, idolatry, sorcery, enmities, strife, jealousy, outbursts of anger, disputes, dissensions, factions, envy, drunkenness, carousing, and "things like these." Paul then notes those who continue to practice such things will not inherit the Kingdom of God. Those were harsh words that likely caused some discomfort to his readers. They should also cause readers today some discomfort. I was in one church meeting where four of these deeds of the flesh were clearly demonstrated.

The Biblical text goes on to contrast the deeds of the flesh with the fruits of the Spirit. Fruit is nourishing and sweet, thus the perfect term to describe the attributes of the Spirit that are demonstrated through love, joy, peace, patience, kindness, goodness, faithfulness, gentleness and self-control. Paul then adds, "...against such there is no law." That last statement is important. "Against such there is no law." There will never be a time when we are unable to choose to exercise the fruits of the Spirit. No law can be passed, no injunction decreed, no Robert's Rule violated by choosing to exercise the fruits of the Spirit.

If your response to conflict manifests deeds of the flesh, you are not embracing grace. Grace can abound even in times of conflict. As I reflect on the contrasting lists of the deeds of the flesh and the fruits of the Spirit, I am not the man I used to be, nor am I the man I hope to become. There is room for all of us to grow, and we will do well to recognize that conflict--whether large or small--is an opportunity to grow in Christlikeness and faith.

As believers, there will be times when the right thing to do is to surrender our rights for the sake of a weaker brother or to preserve unity. There may come times that require standing firm on convictions or calling out an antagonist by name. Know for certain, every believer can respond to conflict without dredging up deeds of the flesh.

If the response to conflict manifests the fruits of the Spirit, you are one step closer to becoming the man or woman who is pleasing to God.

Discussion/Application Questions:

1) What role does grace play in all conflict?
2) How does forgiveness fit into all conflict?
3) What about receiving counsel and advice?
4) Can you list a few thoughts you have taken away from reading this book?
5) Can you list a few action points the Holy Spirit wants you to implement after reading this book?

Helpful Links

http://www.mmsmidwest.com/institute-for-church-management/
    Provider of the *Fireproofing Your Ministry* DVD workshop management training.

http://goodfaithaccounting.com - Accounting, payroll, operational audits, consulting and training for non-profits and churches.

http://www.acfe.com/ The Association of Certified Fraud Examiners. Great place for additional resources in learning about and combating fraud.

http://www.ecfa.org/ The Evangelical Council of Financial Accountability. The Good Housekeeping seal for Christian ministries in how they handle money.

http://www.churchmutual.com All manner of insurance for churches.

https://www.guideone.com/ Church insurance.

http://www.mbts.edu/ Midwestern Baptist Theological Seminary.

http://www.kellerowens.com/not-for-profit-organizations - Many excellent reports, surveys and tools for churches and ministries from a great CPA firm.

Bibliography

Rodney Harrison, Tom Cheyney, Don Overstreet, Spin-Off Churches (Nashville, TN, Broadman & Holman, 2007)

Jeffrey Klick, Love in the Face of Life, (Amazon Digital Services LLC 2018)

Elmer Towns, Getting a Church Started, 3rd ed. (Lynchburg, VA, Liberty University, 1993)

Marlene LeFever, Learning Styles: Reaching Everyone God Gave You to Teach (Colorado Springs, CO, David C. Cook Publishing, 1995)

John Maxwell, Becoming a Person of Influence, (Nashville TN, Thomas Nelson, Inc. 1977)

Gregg Thompson, The Master Coach: Leading with Character, Building Connections, and Engaging in Extraordinary Conversations (Select Books Bluepoint Leadership Series) 2017

Authors

Glenn A. Miller

Glenn has served the Church in multiple capacities since the mid-1980s. Glenn has been a church administrator with two different ministries, CFO of three seminaries, and currently is the CEO of Miller Management Systems, LLC in Kansas City, Missouri, a public accounting firm that serves churches and non-profits exclusively. In addition to training, consulting and offering accounting serving to over 3,000 churches and non-profit organizations, Glenn also founded the Institute for Church Management. Glenn was a highly awarded senior adjunct professor at Baker University for 20 years and has also taught for Sterling College and Avila University. He currently teaches and is a guest lecturer at seminaries in Kansas City. Glenn is a Certified DiSC Personality Assessment Trainer, a Certified Fraud Examiner, and has an MBA from The University of Missouri-KC. He recently completed his Doctorate in Educational Ministries from MBTS. Glenn has been married to Kim since 1981 and has four adult children: Chris, Jon, Beth, and Ben; and, six grandchildren.

Jeffrey A. Klick

Dr. Jeff Klick has been in fulltime church ministry since 1981. He serves as the senior pastor at Hope Family Fellowship in Kansas City, Kansas, a church he planted in 1993. Dr. Klick married his high school sweetheart, Leslie, in May of 1975. They have three adult children and fourteen grandchildren. Dr. Klick loves to learn and has earned a professional designation, Certified Financial Planner, earned a Master's degree in Pastoral Ministry from Liberty Theological Seminary, a Doctorate in Biblical Studies from Master's International School of Divinity, and a Ph.D. in Pastoral Ministry from Trinity Theological Seminary. In addition to serving as senior pastor at Hope Family Fellowship, Dr. Klick is a consultant with The Institute for Church Management and serves on the Board of Directors for The Council for Gospel Legacy Churches. www.jeffklick.com

Rodney Harrison

Dr. Rodney A. Harrison has been in full-time and bi-vocational ministry since 1984. He has taught at Midwestern Baptist Theological Seminary in Kansas City since 2003, where he serves as a Professor of Christian Education and Dean of Postgraduate Studies. Dr. Harrison holds the D.Min. in Mission Administration and a MA in Christian Education from Gateway Baptist Seminary. Harrison and his wife, Julie, have three adult children, Joshua, Cassandra, and Gabrielle. In addition to his role in theological education, he is a higher education and church consultant, conference speaker and curriculum writer.

Thank you for reading our thoughts. We trust God will use this tool to further the work of His Kingdom.

Books and Videos by the Authors

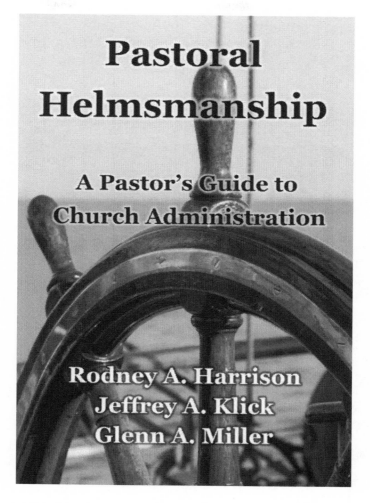

The authors' first book together is rapidly becoming required reading for every pastor and seminary student. Pastors typically will spend 40-60% of their time in administration, yet rarely will they be trained for this expenditure. This book is both a handbook and textbook to help close the gap between training and reality.

Confessions of a Church Felon, book two in our Pastoral Training Series, reveals the inner workings behind the all too typical financial failure of church fraud. Clear, challenging and insightful, Confessions follows the true-life story of a major fraud case. Guaranteed to open your eyes and help save your ministry if the steps within its pages are followed.

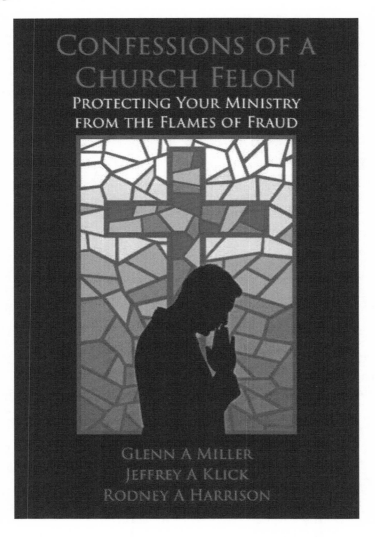

Rodney's Books

Seven Steps for Planting New Churches - One of the first books on church planting written from the perspective of the sponsoring church. *Seven Steps* is a practical guide for pastors and church leaders committed to church multiplication.

Spin-Off Churches: How One Church Successfully Plants Another - This comprehensive resource for sponsoring new congregations available in print and e-book formats.

Jeff's Books (available at Amazon.com in print, audio, or Kindle)

Courage to Flee, Second Edition - How to achieve and keep moral freedom.

Gospel Legacy: A Church and Family Model - God's plan for the family explained from a Biblical perspective.

The Master's Handiwork - God is not finished with any of us yet and He never fails, so don't give up or in.

Reaching the Next Generation for Christ: The Biblical Role of the Family and Church - Detailed research on faith impartation to the next generation.

The Discipling Church: Our Great Commission - An in-depth study and training guide on the Great Commission.

A Glimpse Behind the Calling: The Life of a Pastor - Written to help both pastors and those who love them.

For Our Consideration: Food for the Christian Mind – Sixty devotionals and eight in-depth Bible studies to assist parents, small groups or anyone wanting to dig deep into the Word of God.

Love in the Face of Life – A practical guide to learn how to walk in 1 Corinthians 13 love.

Glenn Videos

3 Hour HD - Workshop DVDs available at
www.mmsmidwest.com/institute-for-church-management

Fireproof Your Ministry! - Installing affordable internal
controls to prevent fraud and increase credibility. A
perfect complement to this book.

*Church Administrator/Treasurer 101: Understanding the
basics of effective church administration* - Required
for everyone dealing with church administration.

~~~~~~

Galatians 6:9 - And let us not grow weary of doing good,
for in due season we will reap, if we do not give up.

Romans 12:18 - If possible, so far as it depends on you,
live peaceably with all.

Philippians 4:7 - And the peace of God, which surpasses
all understanding, will guard your hearts and your
minds in Christ Jesus.

Philippians 2:3 - Do nothing from selfish ambition or
conceit, but in humility count others more significant
than yourselves.

Ephesians 4:31-32 - Let all bitterness and wrath and
anger and clamor and slander be put away from you,
along with all malice. Be kind to one another,
tenderhearted, forgiving one another, as God in Christ
forgave you.

Maranatha!

Made in the USA
Middletown, DE
21 March 2021

35394238R00132